The Go Programming Language Reference

Reference

Definitive Reference for Developers and Engineers

Richard Johnson

Contents

Introduction

This book serves as a comprehensive reference manual for the Go programming language, providing in-depth coverage of its syntax, semantics, and advanced features. It is designed to support both new learners seeking a systematic understanding of Go and experienced developers requiring an authoritative resource for language specifics and best practices.

The language specification presented herein is organized to address the fundamental constructs and abstractions that define Go's programming model. Beginning with the formal description of lexical elements and syntax, the reader is guided through the composition of tokens, literals, operators, and the established formatting conventions. This precise delineation forms the cornerstone for writing syntactically correct and idiomatic Go code.

Building upon this foundation, the treatment of core and composite types elucidates the representation and manipulation of primitive types, strings, arrays, slices, maps, structs, and pointers. Each type is articulated with attention to its memory layout, operational semantics, and usage constraints, enabling programmers to model data structures efficiently and correctly.

The book explores declarations and scope rules in detail, explaining the nuances of variable and constant declarations, type aliases, identifier visibility, package organization, and initialization sequencing. These elements contribute to the modularity and encapsulation mechanisms inherent in Go, supporting the development of maintainable and scalable applications.

Functions, methods, and closures receive thorough examination, including syntax, multiple return values, higher-order functions, method receivers, and control-flow constructs such as defer, panic, and recover. The interaction of these features underpins Go's approach to abstraction and error handling, integral to building robust software.

Interfaces, composition, and reflection form a critical aspect of Go's type system. The exposition covers interface declaration, satisfaction rules, dynamic dispatch, embedding, and runtime inspection via reflection. The discussion includes design recommendations that promote flexible and loosely coupled components, which are conducive to extensible software architecture.

Concurrency and parallelism are principal themes in Go, addressed comprehensively through goroutines, channels, select statements, synchronization primitives, context propagation, memory model, and common concurrency patterns. This section provides the theoretical and practical knowledge necessary to write safe and performant concurrent programs.

Error handling strategies are considered essential for reliability. The book examines errors as values, custom error types, propagation techniques, recoverability distinctions, and testing methodologies. Emphasis is placed on idiomatic patterns that facilitate clear and maintainable error management.

The Go toolchain and build system are presented with an overview of modules, dependency management, compilation, testing, static analysis, and cross-compilation. Readers gain insights into the development ecosystem that supports efficient software delivery and quality assurance.

Lastly, the book addresses advanced language features and runtime aspects, including generics, runtime internals, the unsafe package, foreign function interfaces, advanced reflection use cases, profiling, diagnostics, and language evolution. This content equips readers with a deeper understanding of the capabilities and considerations in leveraging Go to its fullest extent.

Throughout, the book maintains a precise and formal tone, focusing on the specification and practical implications of language constructs. It assumes a foundational familiarity with programming concepts, while providing the necessary rigor and detail to serve as a definitive resource for the Go programming language.

4

Chapter 1

Lexical Elements and Syntax

Dive into the heart of how Go code is structured and read, from the fundamental building blocks to the conventions that empower consistency and productivity. This chapter reveals how Go's seemingly simple syntax choices yield powerful results, promoting clarity without sacrificing expressive power. Discover how even the smallest details—like formatting and comments—are carefully designed to streamline team collaboration and program correctness.

1.1. Tokens and Identifiers

In the Go programming language, tokens form the fundamental building blocks of source code, representing atomic units that the compiler processes during lexical analysis. Understanding tokens and identifiers is crucial for comprehending Go's syntactic structure and for writing code that aligns with its design principles, which emphasize readability, simplicity, and safety.

A token is a sequence of characters that is treated as a single unit in the grammatical structure of a program. Go classifies tokens into several categories: keywords, identifiers, literals, operators, and delimiters. These categories facilitate the language's parsing by providing clear and unambiguous syntactic units.

Go's lexical grammar is designed to be simple and deterministic. The scanner operates on the principle of maximal munch, where the longest possible valid token is always selected from the input stream. This approach eliminates ambiguity when tokenizing code and simplifies error detection by the compiler.

Identifiers in Go are names used to identify variables, constants, types, functions, and other user-defined entities. The rules for forming identifiers reflect a balance between flexibility and clarity, ensuring identifiers are expressive yet unambiguous. The lexical specification states that an identifier must start with a letter or an underscore, followed by any combination of letters, digits, and underscores:

```
identifier = letter { letter | unicode_digit } ;
```

The notion of *letter* includes not only the ASCII letters A-Z and a-z but also Unicode letters, enabling the inclusion of non-ASCII characters for internationalization. Digits are restricted to ASCII digits 0-9, prohibiting digits as the initial character to avoid conflicts with numeric literals.

It is worth noting that while Go allows the use of underscore _ at the beginning and within identifiers, the underscore alone _ serves a special purpose as the blank identifier, a placeholder to discard values.

Examples of valid identifiers include `calculateValue`, `_temp123`, and Unicode-inclusive identifiers like . Invalid identifiers include those starting with digits, e.g., `123abc`, or containing invalid characters such as `$variable`.

6

Go defines a fixed set of reserved keywords that are syntactically significant and cannot be used as identifiers. These keywords represent core language constructs, such as control flow, type declarations, and interface definitions. Their reservation prevents naming conflicts that would otherwise compromise code readability and correctness.

The complete list of Go's reserved keywords is as follows:

break	default	func	interface	select
case	defer	go	map	struct
chan	else	goto	package	switch
const	fallthrough	if	range	type
continue	for	import	return	var

Any attempt to declare identifiers that coincide with these keywords results in a compilation error. This strict separation between keywords and identifiers contributes to the language's lexical simplicity by maintaining a clear, non-overlapping taxonomy of tokens.

One of Go's design philosophies is to reduce the complexity inherent in lexical analysis to minimize ambiguities and unexpected parsing behavior. To this end, the language restricts certain token formations and enforces explicit separations between tokens to prevent accidental merging or misinterpretation.

For example, Go distinguishes operators and delimiters clearly through their syntax, avoiding tokens that could be confused with identifiers or literals. The maximal munch rule plays a central role here: when multiple valid tokens can match the input, the longest valid token is selected, thereby disallowing split or partial tokenings that could lead to errors.

Go also prohibits the use of Unicode digits as identifier characters beyond ASCII digits, which prevents confusions in numeral parsing and word recognition. Furthermore, a space or punctuation character is always required to separate tokens; adjacent tokens that might be confused if concatenated are either disallowed or result in a separate token.

Consider the following snippet:

```
var count int
count := count + 1
```

Here, each token-keyword var, identifier count, keyword int, operator :=, and operator +-is clearly and deterministically recognized by the scanner. The presence of spaces prevents ambiguous readings; for instance, the increment expression count+1 is tokenized as count, +, and 1.

Identifiers in Go are case-sensitive, a feature inherited from its C and Pascal lineage. This sensitivity allows the language to distinguish Value from value as two separate identifiers. Beyond case sensitivity, Go introduces a convention tied to identifier capitalization that implicitly affects visibility at the package level.

Specifically, identifiers that begin with an uppercase letter are exported and hence accessible from other packages, whereas those beginning with a lowercase letter are unexported and package-private. This convention replaces verbose access control syntax found in some languages and integrates lexical rules directly into the lexical and syntactic structures:

```
package mathutils

// Exported identifier because it starts with uppercase
func CalculateArea(radius float64) float64 {
    return 3.14159 * radius * radius
}

// unexported identifier, visible only within package
func helperFunction() {
    // implementation
}
```

This lexical rule facilitates a simple and intuitive packaging system and reduces complexity in symbol table handling during compilation and linking.

By defining a clear and concise specification for tokens and identifiers, Go achieves a disciplined lexical structure that prevents ambiguities and enhances error detection. The combination of reserved keywords, strict identifier formation rules, the maximal munch scanning principle, and case-sensitive exportation conventions coalesce to support Go's aims of simplicity, security, and maintainability. This approach ensures that Go source code remains highly readable while retaining sufficient expressiveness to support complex software engineering tasks.

1.2. Literals and Constants

Literals represent fixed data values embedded directly within source code, serving as explicit expressions of primitive data. Their syntax and semantics form the foundation upon which data manipulation and computation rest. This section elaborates on the variety of literals—numerical, runic, string, and boolean—alongside an examination of constants, emphasizing their declarations, type safety implications, performance considerations, and contribution to code clarity.

Numerical Literals

Numerical literals encompass integer and floating-point values, each adhering to specific syntax patterns representative of their type and magnitude.

Integer literals denote whole numbers without fractional components. They can be specified in several bases: decimal (base 10), hexadecimal (base 16), octal (base 8), and binary (base 2). Prefix conventions differentiate these formats. For example, hexadecimal literals begin with a 0x or 0X, octal with 0o or 0O, and binary with 0b or 0B. Underscores (_) may be interspersed between digits to improve readability, without affecting the literal's value.

```
42              % Decimal integer literal
0x2A            % Hexadecimal literal for decimal 42
0o52            % Octal literal for decimal 42
0b101010        % Binary literal for decimal 42
```

```
1_000_000       % Decimal literal with digit separators
```

Integer literals' semantics involve the implicit or explicit association with a particular integral type—such as int, long, or fixed-width types like int32_t—depending on the context, language rules, and magnitude constraints. Failure to match a literal's magnitude with a compatible type may raise compilation or runtime errors due to overflow.

Floating-point literals represent real numbers incorporating fractional parts and optional exponents. They generally utilize decimal notation with a decimal point and may include scientific notation to denote scale factors.

```
3.14            % Simple floating-point literal
2.0e10          % Scientific notation (2.0 × 10^{10})
0.1             % Fractional value
6.022e23        % Avogadro's number in scientific notation
```

Floating-point literals often default to a language's standard double-precision type unless suffixed or explicitly typed to single precision or extended precision formats. The precision and range of these literals are dictated by the underlying IEEE 754 standard, with rounding and representation errors being important semantic considerations for high-fidelity numerical computations.

Runes

Runes represent Unicode code points as single atomic values and are integral in handling character data beyond basic ASCII. They are typically enclosed in single quotes, distinguishing them from string literals. The literal encompasses a single Unicode scalar value corresponding to a graphical character or control symbol.

```
'a'             % ASCII rune literalΩ
' '             % Greek capital letter omega
'\n'            % Newline character (escape sequence)
'\u03A9'        % Unicode escape sequence for Omega
```

Runes provide precise control over character data through explicit code point representation, facilitating internationalization and text processing where multibyte encoding schemes such as UTF-8 are insufficiently expressive in source code.

String Literals

String literals are sequences of characters enclosed within double quotes (or language-specific delimiters) and represent immutable textual data. They may embed escape sequences for special characters, such as newlines (\n), tabs (\t), and escaped quotes (\").

```
"Hello, World!"      % Simple string literal
"Line1\nLine2"       % String literal with newline escape
"\"Quoted text\""    % String containing quotation marks
"Unicode: \u263A"    % String with Unicode smiley face
```

Some languages support raw string literals, allowing inclusion of special characters without escaping, simplifying the representation of complex strings such as regular expressions or multi-line text. The immutability of string literals ensures integrity and allows optimizations such as interning, minimizing memory footprint and improving performance by reusing identical string instances.

Boolean Literals

Boolean literals are the simplest form of literal, representing the two truth values—true and false. They are used ubiquitously in control flow, logical expressions, and condition evaluation.

```
true     % Boolean literal representing truth
false    % Boolean literal representing falsehood
```

These literals possess an implicit association with the language's boolean type, providing clarity and type safety in conditional constructs while enabling aggressive compiler optimizations due to their fixed, known values.

Constants: Declaration and Usage

Constants are named, immutable values declared through explicit

CHAPTER 1. LEXICAL ELEMENTS AND SYNTAX

syntax, allowing the binding of literals or expressions to identifiers that cannot be modified at runtime. This immutability is fundamental for maintaining integrity, enforcing semantic correctness, and enabling compiler optimizations.

Constants are typically declared using keywords such as `const`, `final`, or `constexpr` depending on the language, followed by an explicit type and initialization expression. For example:

```
const int MaxConnections = 100;
final double Pi = 3.141592653589793;
constexpr int Factorial7 = 5040;
```

The use of constants contrasts with variables, which may be reassigned, allowing the compiler and readers to reason about the program's behavior with stronger invariants.

Constants contribute significantly to type safety by guaranteeing the fixed nature of their values, preventing inadvertent reassignment or mutation. This immutability ensures that once a constant is declared with a precise type, any attempt to assign a value of incompatible type or modify the value is flagged at compile-time, reducing runtime errors.

Assigning frequently used literal values to constants allows compilers to perform constant folding and inlining optimizations, generating efficient machine code. Constants do not incur runtime overhead associated with mutable state, facilitate static analysis, and enable better utilization of CPU caches by representing well-known fixed values.

Constants improve readability and maintainability by replacing magic numbers and strings with meaningful identifiers. This practice aids in documenting intent, reducing duplication, and centralizing value updates.

```
const int DefaultTimeout = 30;     % timeout in seconds

// Instead of hardcoding `30`, using DefaultTimeout:
if (elapsedTime > DefaultTimeout) {
    triggerTimeout();
```

```
}
```

Expressing domain-specific constraints and important numerical values through constants increases the semantic clarity of source code.

Summary of Syntax and Semantics Interactions

The interplay between literals and constants emphasizes the balance between explicit value usage and abstraction via symbolic naming. Literals encode primitive data directly using standardized syntactic forms, whereas constants assign these values to identifiers that enforce immutability and type discipline. Understanding this relationship is crucial for writing robust code where value integrity, correctness, and clarity are paramount.

Moreover, the precise syntax for each literal category ensures the compiler unambiguously interprets source code, while the semantic implications guarantee the right data types and behaviors at runtime. Efficient usage of constants leveraging literals leads to optimized, maintainable, and self-documenting codebases with strong static guarantees.

Mastery of literals and constants lays the groundwork for expressive, performant, and type-safe programming by establishing a reliable medium for data representation and immutability within the source.

1.3. Operators and Precedence

The Go programming language provides a concise and well-defined set of operators designed to facilitate clear, predictable, and efficient expressions. Understanding these operators and their evaluation rules is essential for writing correct and maintainable Go code. This overview details Go's operators, encompassing arithmetic, comparison, logical, and bitwise categories, and examines operator precedence and associativity, which govern evaluation order within expressions.

Arithmetic operators in Go perform fundamental numeric computations:

- + (addition)

- - (subtraction)

- * (multiplication)

- / (division)

- % (modulus, remainder after integer division)

These operators apply to numeric types such as integers, floating-point numbers, and complex numbers. Go does not allow implicit conversions between these types; operands must be explicitly the same type, with any necessary conversions carried out by the programmer to prevent unsafe arithmetic operations.

The division operator / behaves differently depending on operand types: integer division truncates towards zero, while floating-point division produces a floating-point quotient.

Unary arithmetic operators include unary plus (+) and unary minus (-), each applied to a single operand to indicate its sign.

Comparison operators enable relational evaluations and yield boolean results:

- == (equal to)

- != (not equal to)

- < (less than)

- <= (less than or equal to)

- > (greater than)

- >= (greater than or equal to)

These operators are applicable to numeric types, strings, and other types that support comparison, such as pointers and interfaces. Equality comparisons on structs and arrays are allowed only if all their fields or elements are themselves comparable, thereby enforcing type safety and preventing runtime panics.

Comparison expressions always yield a boolean value, true or false, and are typically employed within control constructs.

Logical operators act on boolean operands to facilitate compound logical expressions:

- && (logical AND)

- || (logical OR)

- ! (logical NOT)

These operators are essential for implementing conditional flow. The binary operators && and || implement short-circuit evaluation: the right-hand operand is evaluated only if the left-hand operand does not already determine the result. For example, in a && b, if a is false, then b is not evaluated because the overall expression cannot be true.

The unary operator ! inverts a boolean value, enabling concise negations.

Bitwise operators manipulate individual bits of integer operands:

- & (bitwise AND)

- | (bitwise OR)

- ^ (bitwise XOR)

- & (bit clear, AND NOT)

- << (left shift)

- >> (right shift)

Bitwise AND (&), OR (|), and XOR (^) operate on respective bits of two integers. The bit clear operator & clears bits of the first operand wherever the corresponding bit in the second operand is set, effectively performing an AND-NOT operation.

Shift operators move bits left or right by a specified number of positions: left shifts increase the value by multiplying by a power of two, while right shifts divide (discarding shifted-out bits). Shift counts must be unsigned integers, enforcing explicit intent and preventing issues with negative or excessively large shifts.

Go defines a strict precedence hierarchy to resolve expressions with multiple operators without requiring excessive parentheses. Mastery of precedence is crucial to accurately predict the outcome of expressions and avoid subtle bugs.

The precedence order from highest to lowest is summarized in the table below:

Precedence	Operators
1	Parentheses (), array/slice indexing [], function calls (), selectors ., type assertions
2	Unary operators: +, -, !, ^ (bitwise NOT)
3	Multiplicative: *, /, %, <<, >>, &, &
4	Additive: +, -, |, ^
5	Comparison: ==, !=, <, <=, >, >=
6	Logical AND: &&
7	Logical OR: ||
8	Assignment and short variable declaration

Associativity determines how operators of the same precedence are grouped in the absence of parentheses. All binary operators in Go associate left-to-right, with the exception of unary and assignment operators, which associate right-to-left.

Consider the following example:

16

```
x := 3 + 4 * 5
```

Here, multiplication has higher precedence than addition, so 4 *
5 is evaluated first, resulting in 3 + 20 which equals 23.

Explicit parentheses can override the default precedence, improving clarity or enforcing a specific evaluation order.

Go's operator design emphasizes explicitness, safety, and clarity:

- The lack of implicit type conversions mandates explicit casting, reducing the chance of unintended numerical errors.

- Short-circuiting logical operators prevent unnecessary computation and unwanted side effects.

- The dedicated bit clear operator & communicates its intent more clearly than a combination of AND and NOT.

- Disallowing operator overloading eliminates a class of ambiguities that hinder readability and maintainability.

- Restricting shift counts to unsigned values ensures that negative shift errors cannot occur and enforces vigilant programming.

These features ensure that Go code is predictable and free from hidden implicit behaviors, promoting robust and maintainable software.

In practical terms, arithmetic operators deliver succinct numeric computations, comparison operators facilitate control flow, logical operators enable complex boolean logic with reliable short-circuit semantics, and bitwise operators enable precise manipulation of low-level data-particularly useful in systems programming and performance-sensitive code.

Careful consideration of operator precedence and associativity is vital when combining operators within expressions to avoid logical errors. When in doubt, using parentheses can help reinforce the intended evaluation order and increase code readability.

The minimal and explicit operator set in Go encourages programmers to make deliberate decisions, reducing the potential for subtle mistakes and aligning with Go's principles of simplicity and robustness.

The following example combines multiple operator types to illustrate precedence in practice:

```
var a, b, c int = 5, 10, 3

result := (a + b) << c &^ 0xFF | 1 == 0 && !false
```

The evaluation proceeds as follows:

- Parentheses: calculate a + b to obtain 15

- Shift: 15 << 3 equals 120 (left shift 15 by 3 bits)

- Bit clear: 120 &0xFF results in 0 (clearing all bits of 120 that are set in 0xFF)

- Bitwise OR: 0 | 1 equals 1

- Comparison: 1 == 0 yields false

- Logical AND: false && !false becomes false && true, evaluating to false

This example clearly demonstrates how operator precedence and associativity yield a deterministic result for complex expressions, fostering readability and correctness by design.

1.4. Comments and GoDoc Formatting

In the Go programming language, comments serve not only to enhance code readability but also to facilitate automated documentation generation. Comprehending the nature and best practices of Go comments is essential for producing maintainable and self-explanatory codebases. Go fundamentally supports two forms of comments: line comments and block comments. Each type is purposefully designed for different contexts, and their appropriate usage contributes significantly to clarity and usability.

Line comments begin with a double forward slash // and extend to the end of the line. They are primarily used for brief explanations or clarifications adjacent to code. Their concise nature makes them ideal for inline remarks, clarifying tricky expressions or intentions without interrupting reading flow.

```
func add(a int, b int) int {
    // Return the sum of a and b
    return a + b
}
```

Block comments, enclosed between /* and */, can span multiple lines and are commonly reserved for detailed explanations or temporarily disabling blocks of code during development. However, their usage for inline documentation is generally discouraged in Go to maintain consistency and leverage tooling support that specifically favors line comments.

```
/*
Calculate the factorial of a non-negative integer n.
Uses a recursive approach:
    factorial(n) = n * factorial(n-1)
Base case: factorial(0) = 1
*/
func factorial(n int) int {
    if n == 0 {
        return 1
    }
    return n * factorial(n-1)
}
```

The GoDoc tooling system automates documentation extraction directly from source code comments and relies heavily on a specific commenting convention. GoDoc parses only line comments placed immediately preceding top-level declarations-such as functions, types, variables, and constants. This convention urges developers to write self-contained and descriptive comments starting with the name of the element being documented.

For instance, a function Add should have a comment beginning with Add:

```
// Add returns the sum of two integers.
func Add(a int, b int) int {
    return a + b
}
```

This naming pattern is no mere stylistic preference; it aligns with GoDoc's parsing heuristic to link text and code reliably. Additionally, this style produces natural English sentences for documentation pages, enhancing readability in generated documentation.

Well-written GoDoc comments fulfill dual roles: they educate developers reading source code directly and enable automated tools to produce accurate, user-friendly API documentation. The synergy between source comments and documentation generation promotes synchronization between code and documentation, curtailing discrepancies frequently encountered in traditional manual documentation approaches.

There are further conventions to observe for maximal GoDoc utility:

- Comments should be complete sentences and preferably straightforward and concise.

- Avoid vague or obvious descriptions; instead, emphasize the behavior, purpose, or side effects of the code element.

- For complex functionalities, comments can mention usage examples, though separate example functions often complement this better.

- Do not duplicate information already explicit in function signatures or names; rather, augment understanding in ways code alone cannot communicate.

Package-level comments also follow a strict pattern: a block of line comments should precede the `package` keyword, providing a synopsis of the package's purpose and key functionalities.

```
// Package mathutil provides utility functions for mathematical
    computations,
// including factorial and prime checking.
package mathutil
```

When applied consistently, this system bestows several benefits: it incentivizes developers to clarify design intentions during implementation, ensures users can discover API semantics effortlessly, and seamlessly integrates with ecosystem tools such as godoc and go doc.

Lastly, Go supports the `//go:` directive-style comments used to convey compiler or runtime directives, which are distinct from documentation comments and follow specific syntax rules. Their usage is specialized and is generally avoided outside of critical performance or behavior tuning contexts.

Understanding and embracing Go's comment styles and GoDoc formatting conventions is paramount in crafting codebases that communicate clearly and leverage automated documentation effectively. By writing precise, properly structured comments, developers enable their code to simultaneously serve as executable logic and living documentation that evolves naturally with the software.

1.5. Statement Structure and Blocks

In Go, the fundamental unit of program execution is the statement. Understanding the precise structure of statements and their organization into blocks is essential for writing clear, maintainable code. Unlike some languages that permit varied and complex statement groupings, Go adopts a deliberate, minimalistic syntax that promotes readability and reduces the risk of subtle errors.

A *statement* in Go is a complete instruction-an action or operation to execute. Common categories of statements include expression statements, declaration statements, control statements (such as if, for, and switch), and jump statements (e.g., return, break). Each statement generally ends with an implicit semicolon inserted by the compiler, permitting source code to omit explicit semicolons while maintaining syntactical clarity.

Statements in Go are frequently organized into *blocks*, which are delimited by braces {}. A block acts as a single compound statement that groups multiple statements together, creating a new lexical scope. This lexical scoping is one of the fundamental mechanisms that govern variable visibility and lifetime in Go.

A block always starts with an opening brace and ends with a closing brace. Within these boundaries, statements are executed sequentially. Blocks can nest arbitrarily, allowing complex hierarchical program structures to be expressed clearly.

For example, the body of a function or the branches of conditionals are blocks:

```
func example() {
    var x int = 10
    if x > 5 {
        x = x + 1
    }
    for i := 0; i < x; i++ {
        fmt.Println(i)
    }
}
```

Here, the function body forms a top-level block, the if statement contains a nested block, and the for loop introduces another nested block. Each block defines a new lexical scope, allowing variables declared inside to remain local and limiting their visibility to that block.

The scope created by blocks is critical to prevent name collisions and unintended side effects. For instance, a variable declared inside an `if` block ceases to exist beyond that block:

```
if x := compute(); x > 0 {
    fmt.Println("Positive:", x)
}
// Here, 'x' is not accessible
```

This block-local variable x shadows any variable with the same name in an outer scope, emphasizing the importance of understanding block scopes for correct variable handling.

Go implicitly inserts semicolons at the end of statements, based on simple lexical rules: a semicolon is inserted if the last token on a line is an identifier, basic literal, break, return, or ++/--, among others. This rule allows for clean code without trailing semicolons. However, it also imposes subtleties: line breaks can, in some cases, influence the interpretation of statements, especially when writing multi-line expressions.

One common pitfall arises with `return` statements returning composite literals or function calls split across multiple lines. To avoid unintended semicolon insertion, it is advisable to keep the opening delimiters on the same line as the `return` keyword when returning composite literals:

```
return SomeStruct{
    Field1: value1,
    Field2: value2,
}
```

Breaking the line immediately after `return` can cause the compiler to insert a semicolon prematurely, resulting in syntax errors or unintended behavior.

Go's statements and blocks emphasize minimalism and clarity. For control structures like `if`, `for`, and `switch`, the optional header expressions are tightly defined and must be followed by a single block:

```
if condition {
    // block statements
```

```
}

for i := 0; i < 10; i++ {
    // block statements
}

switch val {
case 1:
    // block statements
default:
    // block statements
}
```

Notably, Go does not support parentheses around conditions or loop headers, reducing syntactic clutter. This design choice improves readability and reduces errors from misplaced parentheses. Additionally, each control structure's body must be a block (even if it contains only a single statement), avoiding ambiguities present in many other languages where braces can be optional.

Within blocks, Go supports grouping declarations of variables, constants, and types. Grouping allows related identifiers to be declared together in a concise and understandable manner:

```
var (
    a int
    b string
    c float64
)

const (
    Pi  = 3.1415
    E   = 2.7182
)
```

Though this grouping mechanism exists at the block scope level, it is syntactic sugar that does not affect runtime behavior. All declarations have their usual scope rules based on the block in which they reside. Grouping helps organize code logically, especially in larger blocks containing multiple related declarations.

Within a block, statements execute sequentially unless a control flow statement modifies the flow. Go's clear-cut approach forbids complex statement groupings glued together by commas or other tokens, a contrast to languages allowing comma-separated expressions or multiple statements on one line.

This strict one-statement-per-line (or per semicolon) policy enhances readability and debuggability, as each statement corresponds directly to an executed action or decision point. Errant commas or misplaced semicolons are thus avoided, and tooling integrates better with this straightforward structure.

This precise model of statements and blocks reduces errors that are often subtle and hard to detect. For example, requiring braces on all control statements avoids the classic *dangling else* problem found in other languages. Local block scope guards against name pollution and unintended variable shadowing. Minimal and consistent semicolon insertion rules diminish syntactic surprises.

Together, these design choices enable Go programs to be easier to read, analyze, and maintain. They align well with Go's goal of simplicity and clarity in source code, directly improving developer productivity and program correctness.

Through a disciplined yet minimal statement and block structure, Go provides a robust foundation for writing expressive, safe, and legible systems programs.

1.6. Whitespace, Formatting, and GoFmt

Go distinguishes itself from many programming languages by enforcing strict yet straightforward rules regarding whitespace and formatting, thereby fostering a uniform code style across diverse development environments. Unlike languages that allow a broad range of stylistic choices, Go's design philosophy regards source code formatting as a solvable, machine-handled problem rather than one of subjective preference. The primary mechanism for this enforcement is the `gofmt` tool, which automatically formats Go source code according to a standardized style.

At the language specification level, Go defines whitespace and formatting rules that influence how tokens are recognized and interpreted during lexical analysis. For instance, Go uses semicolons to terminate statements but inserts them automatically during scanning, based on explicit newline rules. This automatic semicolon insertion depends on the placement of whitespace and newline characters, enforcing specific constraints such that developers naturally write lines adhering to the language's syntax expectations without manually typing semicolons. This behavior regularizes statement termination and reduces syntactic noise, making Go code visually cleaner and easier to parse mentally.

Whitespace in Go is not merely aesthetic; it directly impacts tokenization and parsing. Excessive or inconsistent spacing is normalized by the compiler and gofmt, eliminating ambiguity and divergent style variants. Tabs and spaces, while both permitted, are used consistently: gofmt enforces tab-based indentation rather than spaces, reflecting a deliberate choice prioritizing efficient cursor movement and alignment in editors optimized for tab characters. This uniformity aids in avoiding subtle bugs and errors resulting from inconsistent indentation, especially in nested block structures.

The tool gofmt epitomizes Go's approach to code formatting. It reads Go source files and rewrites them in a canonical style that adheres strictly to the language specification's formatting rules. Beyond mere cosmetic adjustments, gofmt ensures that the code's syntactic structure and idiomatic style are preserved, while all extraneous and inconsistent whitespace is normalized. It handles indentation, line breaks, spacing around operators, alignment of declarations, and structuring of composite literals uniformly, producing output that is both human-readable and machine-consistent.

One of the core rationales behind integrating gofmt into the Go development process is to eliminate debates over code style conventions. Traditional software projects often spend considerable time penalizing differing stylistic preferences during code reviews or forcing contributors to manually align with project style guidelines. With gofmt, formatting is fully automated, independent of individual taste, which shifts the focus of code review from stylistic concerns to substantive design and logic considerations. This expedites development workflows, reduces friction during collaboration, and improves merge confidence in version control systems.

Moreover, gofmt tightly integrates with the Go toolchain and popular editors, enabling continuous formatting as source code is written or committed. This integration prevents the accumulation of style inconsistencies within large codebases, ensuring that all code conforms to the same formatting specification and removing the need for style enforcement scripts or manual inspections. The consistent presentation also facilitates the use of automated refactoring tools and static analysis utilities, which rely on well-defined code structures to perform their tasks accurately.

Consider the following example, illustrating how gofmt transforms a snippet of Go code with inconsistent spacing and line breaks into a canonical form:

```
package main
import  "fmt"
func main( ) {
fmt.Println(   "Hello,      world!")
}
```

Applying gofmt to this code yields:

```
package main

import "fmt"

func main() {
    fmt.Println("Hello, world!")
}
```

In this output, note the removal of unnecessary spaces within the func declaration, the insertion of standard line breaks between package declaration, imports, and main function, and the consistent tab indentation of the function body. The `fmt.Println` call's argument, previously spaced irregularly, is trimmed to a single space between words, reflecting idiomatic Go formatting.

The impact of `gofmt` extends beyond aesthetics. Code reviews and merges in large teams benefit from the reduced variability in formatting, as differences highlighted by version control systems more accurately reflect semantic changes rather than whitespace or styling. This leads to faster and more reliable code reviews, lowering cognitive load on reviewers.

Whitespace and formatting rules also influence error detection. Consistent indentation and line structuring help prevent subtle logical errors that arise in languages sensitive to whitespace, such as Python, by making block structures and scopes immediately apparent. While Go does not rely on indentation for semantics, maintaining uniformly formatted code enhances readability, thus indirectly aiding error recognition and troubleshooting.

Go's commitment to a single, opinionated formatting style exemplified by `gofmt` reflects a broader principle: code readability and maintainability are paramount and can be mechanically enforced to reduce human error and style debates. Enforced whitespace rules and automated formatting democratize code contributions, allowing new and experienced developers to produce consistent code without investing effort in formatting decisions. The result is an ecosystem where collaboration, code review, and maintenance are accelerated and clarified by a shared, machine-enforced style standard.

Go's whitespace and formatting design choices, epitomized by the `gofmt` tool, represent a deliberate engineering trade-off: sacrificing personal stylistic freedom to achieve a collective gain in code clarity, defect reduction, and collaborative efficiency. Understanding and embracing these enforced conventions is crucial for proficient Go development and effective participation in Go-based projects.

Chapter 2

Core Types and Composite Types

Unlock the expressive potential of Go's type system—from the raw power of primitives to the flexibility of composite constructs. This chapter demystifies how Go represents and manages data, and why its approach to typing leads to fast, robust, and maintainable programs. Venture beyond simple variables to discover the structure and philosophy behind real-world data in Go.

2.1. Primitive Data Types

At the foundation of Go's type system lie the primitive data types, which serve as the essential building blocks for all variables and expressions within a program. The core primitive types include numeric types (integers and floating-point numbers), boolean types, and the rune type. These types are rigorously defined to ensure precise representation, consistent size guarantees across platforms, and idiomatic performance characteristics. A thorough understanding of these primitives is critical for designing efficient, correct, and idiomatic Go programs.

Go provides a comprehensive suite of numeric types subdivided into signed and unsigned integers, and floating-point numbers. The integer types in Go are distinguished by their bit widths: int8, int16, int32, int64 for signed integers, and uint8, uint16, uint32, uint64 for unsigned integers. Crucially, the type aliases int and uint serve as platform-dependent representations commonly mapped to either 32 or 64 bits depending on the target architecture, favoring the native word size for performance.

Each integer type occupies exactly the number of bytes implied by its bit width, a decision that facilitates deterministic memory layout and predictable interfacing with hardware and system calls. For example, int32 and uint32 consume 4 bytes with two's complement representation for signed integers. Overflows in these types wrap around modulo 2^n, where n is the bit width, which should be carefully managed or explicitly handled in performance-critical applications.

Floating-point types in Go, float32 and float64, adhere to the IEEE-754 standard, ensuring portability and predictable numerical behavior. float64 is preferred for general use due to its superior precision and range, unless memory constraints or interface requirements necessitate float32. The Go runtime guarantees consistent results across platforms, an important consideration for numeric algorithms requiring reproducibility.

The boolean type bool represents truth values with only two possible states: true and false. It is a distinct primitive type that is not interchangeable with numeric types, enforcing type safety at compile time and preventing erroneous logical operations. Internally, a bool occupies one byte, though only a single bit is logically necessary; the additional storage is a tradeoff favoring alignment and efficient access.

In high-performance scenarios, boolean values often participate directly in conditional branching and bitwise manipulations. While Go does not implicitly convert booleans to integers, explicit conversion or patterned constructs (such as ternary-like expressions using if statements) allow effective use of booleans in performance-critical code without sacrificing clarity or correctness.

The rune type in Go is an alias for int32 and embodies a Unicode code point. Unlike raw bytes, which represent arbitrary 8-bit values, runes abstract the representation of textual characters as per the Unicode standard. This abstraction allows Go to operate correctly over Unicode strings, facilitating internationalization and diverse character sets.

A rune value always holds a valid Unicode scalar value or an error substitute such as the replacement character U+FFFD. Go's native support for UTF-8 encoded strings means that runes must often be decoded from or encoded to UTF-8 sequences, which are variable-length and not fixed-width. The consistent 32-bit size of runes provides a uniform representation for characters internally. This is especially useful in algorithms performing character-by-character processing, where clarity and correctness are paramount.

Go's design enforces strict size guarantees for its primitive types to enable predictable program behavior and seamless cross-platform compatibility. The fixed-width integer and floating-point types ensure that programs behave deterministically regardless of the underlying hardware.

For int and uint, the platform-dependent size aligns with the native word size, favoring performance and integration with system-level APIs. Programmers targeting specific size constraints should prefer the explicitly sized types to avoid ambiguity. This design balances flexibility with explicitness: developers can rely on int for general purpose but switch to sized types when precision or external interface compliance matters.

By contrast, `bool` and `rune` carry fixed sizes independent of platform word size, underpinning consistent semantics in logical operations and text processing respectively. These guarantees simplify reasoning about memory layout, data serialization, and interoperation with external systems that expect standardized types.

Effective utilization of primitive types is pivotal in high-performance Go programs. Numeric types directly map to machine instructions and CPU registers, especially when aligned with the machine's word size. For instance, arithmetic involving `int64` on 64-bit architectures is generally efficient, while narrower types may impose additional instructions for sign extension or zero padding.

Avoiding unnecessary conversions between types reduces overhead and enables the compiler to apply aggressive optimizations, such as loop unrolling and vectorization. In performance-sensitive loops, mixing sizes should be avoided since implicit or explicit casts can hamper instruction pipelining and increase register pressure.

Boolean values, while scarce in memory footprint, frequently influence control flow. Branch prediction sensitivity in CPUs means that arranging conditional statements with predictable branching patterns can have more significant performance effects than the raw size of the `bool` type itself.

The `rune` type, being an integer under the hood, can be efficiently manipulated with standard arithmetic and bitwise operations, yet it must be used judiciously in text processing pipelines to avoid costly decoding steps. Performance gains often result from careful batching of UTF-8 decoding or by leveraging Go's built-in libraries optimized in assembly for string iteration.

Type	Size	Range/Characteristics	Typical Usage
int8, int16, int32, int64	1, 2, 4, 8 bytes	Signed integers, two's complement	Precise-width integer operations, interfacing with hardware
uint8, uint16, uint32, uint64	1, 2, 4, 8 bytes	Unsigned integers	Bitwise operations, memory mapping, and network protocols
int, uint	Platform dependent (4 or 8 bytes)	Native word size	General-purpose integer computations
float32, float64	4, 8 bytes	IEEE-754 floating points	Scientific computation, graphics, and physics simulations
bool	1 byte	true or false	Control flow, logical conditions
rune (int32)	4 bytes	Unicode code points	Unicode-compliant text processing

The primitive data types in Go provide a robust yet flexible foundation for both system-level programming and application development. Their strict size guarantees, clear semantic delineation, and tight coupling to hardware and language runtime underpin Go's reputation for writing efficient, reliable, and portable code. Mastery over these primitives enables developers to optimize performance-critical paths and maintain clarity and correctness in all computational domains.

2.2. Strings and Runes

Go's approach to string handling is grounded in the principles of immutability, Unicode-awareness, and simplicity, providing a robust foundation for modern text processing. A string in Go is a read-only slice of bytes, representing a sequence of UTF-8 encoded code units. This design choice marries performance with correctness, allowing the efficient manipulation of Unicode text while preventing accidental modification of string data.

Each Go string is immutable, meaning once created, its byte content cannot be changed. This immutability simplifies reasoning about program behavior, aids compiler optimization, and improves safety by avoiding side effects from concurrent access. Internally, strings are implemented as a struct containing a pointer to a byte array and an integer length, enabling constant-time length retrieval and slice operations without copying. However, it is critical to note that the length returned by `len()` reflects the number of bytes, not the number of Unicode characters or human-perceived symbols.

Because Go strings are UTF-8 encoded, characters outside the ASCII range may occupy multiple bytes. This variable-length encoding introduces complexity in indexing and iteration: direct byte indexing can lead to invalid character boundaries and unexpected results if the string contains multi-byte characters. For instance, consider the string `"café"`—the letter "é" is represented using two bytes in UTF-8, and naive indexing can split the character, producing invalid or incorrect output.

To offer explicit control over Unicode text, Go provides the `rune` data type, an alias for `int32`, representing a single Unicode code point. When iterating over a string with a `for range` loop, Go decodes UTF-8 sequences into individual runes automatically, delivering both the byte index and the decoded code point. This facilitates safe and accurate character-wise processing without manual decoding overhead. For example:

```
s := "Hello,  "
for i, r := range s {
    fmt.Printf("Byte index %d: rune %q\n", i, r)
}
```

The output enumerates Unicode characters rather than raw bytes, which is indispensable for tasks that depend on text semantics, such as parsing, sorting, or case-insensitive comparisons.

Under the hood, the distinction between byte and rune is fundamental. Bytes represent low-level storage units, while runes ab-

34

stract the conceptual "character" visible to users, consistent with Unicode standards. However, it is essential to understand that a rune corresponds to a single Unicode code point, which may not align perfectly with human-perceived characters. Grapheme clusters—user-visible characters that may combine multiple code points (for example, base letters plus diacritics)—require specialized libraries and are beyond Go's standard string facilities.

Explicit conversion from strings to rune slices and vice versa allows bulk operations on Unicode code points. For instance, converting a string to []rune decodes the entire UTF-8 sequence into a slice of code points, enabling index-based access:

```
runes := []rune(s)
fmt.Printf("Second rune: %c\n", runes[1])
```

While this conversion simplifies character-level manipulation, it incurs allocation and decoding cost proportional to string length. Therefore, it should be employed judiciously when direct iteration is insufficient or random access is required for Unicode characters.

Encoding decisions bear heavily on correctness and safety in multilingual applications. Using UTF-8 as the default string encoding aligns Go with the broader ecosystem and the inherently Unicode-compliant format of network protocols, file systems, and many data formats. This universality avoids ambiguity and minimizes the risk of corruption across components. When interacting with legacy or non-UTF-8 data, conversion libraries such as x/text/encoding enable safe transcoding, preserving the integrity of textual information.

Errors in encoding handling, such as treating arbitrary byte sequences as strings without validation, can lead to panics, data loss, or security vulnerabilities. For instance, functions that rely on character boundaries will malfunction if input strings are not valid UTF-8. Consequently, Go's standard library methods often assume UTF-8 validity and advocate explicit validation or sanitization when working with external data sources, reinforcing robustness.

Additional utilities support normalization, casefolding, and colla-
tion tailored to Unicode semantics, crucial for internationalized
applications. However, the core string and rune model establishes
the foundation by ensuring that textual data is consistently represented, correctly interpreted, and efficiently processed.

Go's string model—immutable, UTF-8 encoded, and Unicode-
aware, complemented by the rune type—strikes a balance
between low-level control and high-level convenience. Mastering
this duality is vital for developing applications that are both
performant and correct in a globally diverse software landscape.

2.3. Arrays and Slices

Go provides a dual approach to handling sequential data through
fixed-length *arrays* and dynamically sized *slices*. Both structures
offer distinct advantages for memory management and performance, with slices serving as the idiomatic container for most use
cases, while arrays provide stringent length guarantees essential
for certain algorithmic and interfacing contexts.

An *array* in Go is a contiguous block of memory containing elements of a single type with a fixed size known at compile time. The
declaration syntax for an array of length n and element type T is

```
var a [n]T
```

or equivalently,

```
a := [n]T{elements}
```

where n is a constant integer value. The length of an array is a part
of its type, making [5]int and [10]int distinct types that cannot
be directly assigned or compared without conversion or iteration.

Arrays are value types; assigning one array to another copies all
elements. This implies that passing an array to a function transfers

a copy unless explicitly passed by reference. For large arrays, this may induce performance overhead, motivating the use of slices for most practical manipulations.

Slices are more flexible, representing a segment or window into an underlying array. Conceptually, a slice consists of three components:

- A pointer to the first element of the underlying array included in the slice,

- The length, or number of accessible elements,

- The capacity, defining the total number of elements in the underlying array starting from the first slice element.

The slice type is declared as

```
var s []T
```

which does not allocate storage but defines a reference to an array segment. Slices are dynamically sized and resizable, though the resizing operation depends on the capacity constraint and may necessitate allocating a new underlying array.

Creating a slice can be done in several ways:

```
var a [5]int = [5]int{1, 2, 3, 4, 5}
var s []int = a[1:4]  // slice elements: a[1], a[2], a[3]
```

Here, s refers to the subarray {2, 3, 4}, sharing the memory of a from index 1 up to but not including 4. The slicing expression a[low:high] creates a slice starting at low and extending up to high - 1. The length of the slice is high - low, and its capacity is len(a) - low.

It is important to note that slices may be re-sliced or appended to, modifying their length and potentially triggering allocation if the capacity is exceeded. The append built-in function handles this behavior:

```
s = append(s, 6, 7)
```

If s has sufficient capacity, the new elements are added to the underlying array without allocation; otherwise, a new array is allocated, data is copied, and s now points to the new memory. This technique ensures efficient amortized performance in dynamic array growth scenarios.

Slices must be handled cautiously to avoid dangling references to large underlying arrays when only a small part is needed. For instance, retaining a slice that references a small segment of a large array can prevent garbage collection of the entire array, leading to memory leaks. To mitigate this, it is often advisable to copy slices explicitly when retaining only a subset for longer-term use:

```
smallCopy := make([]int, len(s))
copy(smallCopy, s)
```

Memory backing for slices is a key abstraction. Since slices share storage, modifying a slice element affects the underlying array and other slices referencing the same memory region. This enables efficient data manipulation without redundant copying but requires careful synchronization in concurrent environments.

Accessing elements beyond the slice bounds results in a run-time panic, so robust error handling or bounds checking is essential when indices are derived from dynamic sources. Unlike arrays, slice length can be queried at run-time via the built-in len() function:

```
length := len(s)
capacity := cap(s)
```

The cap() function returns the maximum possible length the slice could grow to without reallocation.

Best practices for error-free and efficient use include:

- Prefer slices over arrays unless fixed-length, compile-time constants are required.

- Use slicing expressions liberally for subsetting without copying, but copy slices when long-term independent storage is needed.

- Avoid assumptions about slice capacities; always check and handle allocation on append.

- Use `make` to initialize slices with explicit length and capacity when performance or memory layout is critical.

- Be aware of shared backing arrays when passing slices across API boundaries or goroutines, ensuring synchronization if modified concurrently.

- Employ zero-value slices (`nil` slices) when no underlying array is needed, as many standard library functions treat nil slices equivalently to empty slices.

Example illustrating array versus slice distinctions:

```
func sumArray(a [3]int) int {
    total := 0
    for _, v := range a {
        total += v
    }
    return total
}

func sumSlice(s []int) int {
    total := 0
    for _, v := range s {
        total += v
    }
    return total
}

arr := [3]int{1, 2, 3}
slice := arr[:]
fmt.Println(sumArray(arr))  // Outputs 6
fmt.Println(sumSlice(slice)) // Outputs 6
```

Here, `sumArray` requires an exact array size and value semantics, while `sumSlice` accepts arbitrary-length dynamic input, reflecting the general preference for slice parameters.

Understanding the nuanced differences and interplay between arrays and slices is foundational for performant, idiomatic Go programming, enabling efficient memory usage, flexible data processing, and robust system design.

2.4. Maps: Internals and Semantics

Maps in Go are the primary associative container, providing an efficient, built-in mechanism for key-value storage. Internally, maps are implemented as hash tables optimized for both speed and memory usage, making them crucial data structures for a wide variety of applications ranging from caching to indexing.

A map in Go is declared using the syntax `map[KeyType]ValueType`. Creation can be performed either by literal initialization, such as `m := map[string]int{"a": 1}`, or by the `make` function, `m := make(map[string]int, 100)`, where the optional second argument specifies a capacity hint that aids internal memory allocation but does not restrict growth.

Key Restrictions and Equality

A fundamental requirement for map keys is that they must be comparable since keys are internally hashed and compared for equality. This excludes types such as slices, maps, and functions from being used as map keys. Acceptable key types include all basic types such as integers, floats, strings, pointers, channels, and structs or arrays composed exclusively of comparable fields. The equality semantics adhere to the `==` operator behavior, ensuring consistent key comparison.

Attempting to use a non-comparable type as a map key results in a compile-time error. Struct keys are compared field-by-field, which enforces consistent and predictable key behavior. It is important to avoid types where equality semantics do not align with intended key use, as this can lead to subtle bugs or unexpected map behavior.

Iteration Order

Go's map iteration order is intentionally randomized. When iterating over a map using `for key, value := range map` syntax, the order of traversal is not specified and varies between iterations. This randomization prevents programmers from relying on any deterministic order, which encourages development of order-independent logic and allows internal optimizations without exposing implementation details.

For deterministic order, explicit sorting of keys is required. The standard pattern to achieve this involves collecting map keys into a slice, sorting the slice with `sort` package functions, and then iterating over the sorted keys. This approach adds overhead but guarantees reproducibility and clarity when order is essential.

Memory Behavior and Allocation

Internally, Go maps employ a hash table with open addressing. Each map contains a descriptor referencing an array of buckets where key-value pairs reside. Buckets store multiple key-value pairs to reduce collisions and improve locality. As the map grows, the runtime dynamically resizes and rehashes entries into a larger bucket array to maintain efficient access times, with typical amortized complexity close to $O(1)$.

The `make` function's capacity hint influences the initial bucket count, allowing for more efficient memory allocations when the approximate map size is known at creation. However, exceeding this capacity triggers a resize operation, which is costly in CPU time and leads to a temporary increased memory footprint. Consequently, pre-sizing maps is a critical optimization in performance-sensitive code paths.

Garbage collection safety is ensured because Go's runtime keeps track of allocated map buckets and entries, avoiding memory leaks even when keys or values contain pointers. However, over-allocating or creating many short-lived maps can increase GC pressure.

Advanced Usage Patterns and Performance Considerations

- **Reuse Maps and Clear Instead of Recreate:** Frequently creating and discarding maps leads to increased garbage collector overhead. Instead, clearing map entries by iterating and deleting keys with `delete(map, key)` allows reuse of internal allocations.

- **Avoid Complex Struct Keys for Frequent Updates:** While using structs as keys is supported, complex or large structs may cause significant computational overhead during key comparison and hashing. In such cases, consider using simpler primitive keys or precomputed hash keys.

- **Beware of Interface Keys:** Maps with interface keys introduce additional indirection and dynamic type checks on equality and hashing, slowing down map operations. Where possible, use concrete types as keys.

- **Minimize Map Resizing:** When possible, estimate the expected map size and initialize it with `make(map[KeyType]ValueType, capacity)` to reduce resize operations.

- **Optimize Iteration:** Because iteration order is random, avoid logic that implicitly depends on it. For complex traversals, extract keys into a slice and sort ahead of map access.

- **Use Maps for Sparse Data:** Maps perform best when data is sparse or dynamically sized. For dense datasets with fixed keys, arrays or slices may be more memory- and CPU-efficient.

Zero Value and Concurrent Access

A map's zero value is `nil`, which behaves like an empty map for lookups (returning zero values) but causes runtime panic on insertion or deletion. Explicit initialization via literals or `make` must precede modification to avoid such panics.

Maps are **not** safe for concurrent use by multiple goroutines without synchronization. Concurrent writes or a mix of reads and writes require explicit locking (e.g., `sync.Mutex`) or usage of concurrent-safe alternatives such as `sync.Map`. Failure to synchronize leads to data races and undefined runtime behavior.

Example: Efficient Map Usage

```
type User struct {
    ID   int
    Name string
}

func processUsers(users []User) map[int]string {
    // Preallocate map with capacity to minimize resizes
    userMap := make(map[int]string, len(users))

    for _, u := range users {
        userMap[u.ID] = u.Name
    }
    return userMap
}

func sortedKeys(m map[int]string) []int {
    keys := make([]int, 0, len(m))
    for k := range m {
        keys = append(keys, k)
    }
    sort.Ints(keys)
    return keys
}

func clearMap(m map[int]string) {
    for k := range m {
        delete(m, k)
    }
}
```

The code snippet demonstrates efficient map creation with preallocation, safe population, retrieval of sorted keys for deterministic iteration, and the recommended approach to clear map entries to facilitate reuse, thereby optimizing both memory and CPU usage.

Mastery of Go's map semantics and internals is vital for writing performant and idiomatic Go programs. Understanding key constraints, iteration behavior, memory patterns, and synchronization requirements empowers developers to utilize maps effectively in concurrent, high-throughput environments.

2.5. Structs: Types, Composition, and Alignment

Structs are fundamental constructs in many programming languages, enabling the modeling of complex data through a composite of multiple fields, each potentially of distinct types. This composition-rich structure allows developers to represent real-world entities and application-specific abstractions with clarity and precision. Understanding the declaration, composition, and alignment of structs is essential for designing scalable and efficient data models.

A struct consists of named fields, each associating a unique identifier with a specific data type. The declaration syntax varies by language, but conceptually, a struct S with fields $f_1, f_2, \ldots$ of types $T_1, T_2, \ldots$ captures a fixed layout:

$$S = \{f_1 : T_1, f_2 : T_2, \ldots, f_n : T_n\}$$

Each field can be accessed using the dot notation, e.g., $s.f_i$. The strong typing of fields enforces correctness in data manipulation, preventing inadvertent operations on incompatible types.

Anonymous fields and embedding provide a mechanism beyond simple named fields. Many languages allow anonymous fields, commonly referred to as struct embedding. Embedding enables one struct to include another struct or type without explicit naming, effectively promoting the embedded type's fields to the outer struct's namespace. This grants a form of inheritance or composition that simplifies struct extension and reuse.

For example, consider embedding a struct `Address` into a struct `Employee`:

```
struct Address {
    char street[50];
    char city[50];
    int zip;
};

struct Employee {
    int id;
    char name[100];
    struct Address;   // anonymous struct field (embedding)
};
```

In this scenario, fields of `Address` behave as if they belong directly to `Employee`. Accessing the `city` field is as direct as `employee.city`, without an explicit intermediate field name. This technique reduces verbosity and enhances the expressiveness of APIs by logically combining types while preserving their identities.

Embedding can also be used to implement polymorphic designs or to add cross-cutting concerns like logging or metadata without modifying existing struct definitions.

The physical layout of a struct in memory profoundly impacts performance, interoperability, and correctness, especially when interfacing with hardware or external systems. Memory alignment refers to how data is arranged and accessed in memory according to the processor's memory access rules, typically requiring that primitive types align on addresses that are multiples of their size or a platform-specific alignment constraint.

45

Each field within a struct must respect alignment boundaries, potentially introducing padding bytes to maintain this alignment. Consider a simple struct with fields of differing sizes:

```
struct Example {
    char a;      // 1 byte
    int b;       // 4 bytes
    short c;     // 2 bytes
};
```

On a platform where int is 4-byte aligned, the memory layout is likely:

a (1 byte)+3 bytes padding+b (4 bytes)+c (2 bytes)+2 bytes padding

Thus, the total size of the struct may be 12 bytes instead of the naive sum of its field sizes (7 bytes) due to these padding requirements. Compilers usually automatically introduce padding to align fields according to processor architecture constraints, improving access efficiency.

Being aware of alignment and padding helps optimize memory footprint and access speed. Grouping fields from largest to smallest can reduce padding, and language-specific directives or attributes can sometimes override default alignment behavior to achieve packed or platform-defined layouts.

Scalable data modeling with structs involves thoughtfully combining primitive types, other structs, pointers or references, and embedding. Key strategies include:

- **Modularity through embedding**: Use anonymous fields to compose complex types hierarchically. For example, embedding Timestamp or Metadata structs into multiple domain entities promotes code reuse and consistency.

- **Encapsulation of logically related fields**: Group fields that belong together into nested structs. This not only provides semantic clarity but also enables partial updates and more manageable data access patterns.

- **Optimizing field ordering**: Arrange fields to minimize padding and improve cache utilization. Typically, ordering from largest to smallest aligned type yields compact layouts. Awareness of the target platform's alignment constraints is critical here.

- **Opaque pointers for decoupling**: Use pointers or references within structs to abstract away complex substructures or variable-sized data. This enables flexibility and prevents unnecessary copying while maintaining a clear and manageable memory model.

- **Avoiding deep nesting complexity**: While nesting improves clarity, excessively deep struct hierarchies increase access cost and complicate serialization or interoperability. Balancing depth and breadth is a design decision based on application context.

Finally, automated tools or language features like reflection, metaprogramming, or code generation can facilitate the maintenance of complex struct-based models, allowing seamless updates and reducing boilerplate.

Mastery of struct types, embedding, and alignment enables the design of robust, efficient, and maintainable data models tailored to complex modern applications. The interplay between type composition and memory layout must be carefully managed to achieve scalable expressiveness without sacrificing performance.

2.6. Pointers and Memory

Pointers in Go offer a controlled and safe mechanism to reference memory locations, enabling efficient low-level programming while maintaining strong safety guarantees imposed by the language's runtime. Unlike in traditional systems programming languages such as C or C++, Go's pointer model restricts direct pointer arithmetic and enforces the use of references through explicit types, balancing expressive power with memory safety.

A pointer in Go is defined using the * operator, denoting a variable that holds the address of a value of a specific type. For example:

```
var p *int      // p is a pointer to an int
var i int = 42
p = &i          // p holds the address of i
```

In this snippet, p points to the memory location of i. Dereferencing p via *p accesses the value stored at that address. This model avoids exposing raw arbitrary memory manipulation, since pointers are always typed and bound to valid data structures.

The zero value of a pointer is nil, indicating that it currently references no valid memory location:

```
var ptr *string  // ptr is nil by default
if ptr == nil {
    // safe to check before dereferencing
}
```

The presence of the zero value is crucial for safe handling of pointers, allowing explicit checks to avoid runtime panics due to dereferencing non-initialized or invalid pointers.

Allocation of memory in Go is primarily performed through two built-in functions: new and make. Both serve allocation purposes but target different kinds of data types and have distinct behaviors.

Allocation with new

The new function allocates zeroed storage for a specified type and returns a pointer to it. It is fundamentally a memory allocator for single values or structures:

```
p := new(int)   // p is *int pointing to zeroed int memory
*p = 27         // assign value through pointer
```

The allocated memory is initialized to the zero value for its type, guaranteeing deterministic initialization and preventing undefined behavior. Use of new is prevalent when a program requires a pointer to a fresh, zeroed instance rather than a stack-allocated value. It is important to note that new does not perform initialization beyond zeroing; manual assignment is necessary for specific values.

Allocation with make

In contrast, make is specialized for initializing slices, maps, and channels. These types require internal runtime structures and dynamic allocation, which make abstracts:

```
s  := make([]int, 5, 10)  // slice of length 5, capacity 10
m  := make(map[string]int)
ch := make(chan int, 2)
```

Unlike new, make returns an initialized value, not a pointer; the returned value is ready for use immediately. Attempting to use new for these composite types yields a pointer to uninitialized runtime structures, generally causing runtime errors if not properly configured.

Safe Interaction with Garbage Collection

Go's runtime includes an advanced garbage collector (GC) that automatically manages memory lifetimes without requiring explicit deallocation by the programmer. When a pointer references an object, the GC tracks it to ensure memory is not reclaimed prematurely. This behavior is critical to avoiding dangling pointers and use-after-free bugs endemic to manual memory management languages.

Pointers to heap-allocated objects are maintained and scanned by the GC, preserving objects when references persist. For example:

```
type Node struct {
    Value int
    Next  *Node
}
```

```
head := &Node{Value: 1}      // allocated on heap
head.Next = &Node{Value: 2}  // garbage collector tracks
    both nodes
```

Here, nodes linked by pointers are allocated on the heap, and the GC automatically manages their lifetimes as long as head or subsequent nodes are reachable. This model enables dynamic data structures such as linked lists, trees, and graphs with minimal programmer overhead.

Balancing Power and Safety

Go restricts pointer arithmetic severely, prohibiting pointer incrementing or arbitrary manipulation common in C. This design prevents undefined behavior and enhances memory safety. Instead, Go encourages expressive use of slices and maps for most data manipulations. Nonetheless, explicit pointers retain power when direct reference semantics or mutable shared state are necessary.

For example, mutation through pointers is straightforward:

```
func increment(ptr *int) {
    *ptr++
}

var x int = 10
increment(&x)      // x is now 11
```

This capability ensures efficient updates without copying large data structures.

Furthermore, Go's pointer model integrates seamlessly with interfaces and method receivers, allowing both value and pointer receiver semantics to precisely control method behavior and memory usage patterns.

- Pointers are typed references to memory locations and can be nil by default.

- new allocates zeroed memory for any type and returns a

pointer to it.

- make initializes slices, maps, and channels, returning initialized values rather than pointers.

- Garbage collection tracks pointer references, allowing for safe automatic memory management.

- Pointer arithmetic is disallowed to prevent unsafe memory access.

- Pointers enable efficient mutation and reference sharing while preserving memory safety.

This pointer methodology in Go forms a robust foundation for effective systems programming, delivering a well-balanced approach that safeguards low-level memory interactions without sacrificing expressiveness or performance.

Chapter 3

Declarations and Scope

Explore the hidden architecture beneath Go programs: how names, values, and types are introduced and controlled across packages, files, and functions. This chapter unpacks the subtle scoping rules, initialization order, and declaration forms that underpin Go's renowned scalability and code clarity—empowering you to write code that's not just correct, but also elegant and maintainable.

3.1. Variable and Constant Declarations

Go provides a rich and flexible set of constructs for declaring variables and constants, each designed to serve particular programming needs and to optimize code readability, safety, and performance. Understanding these techniques is crucial for writing clear and efficient Go programs and managing scope and initialization semantics carefully.

53

The primary mechanism for declaring variables in Go is the `var` keyword. A `var` declaration may specify a type explicitly or allow the compiler to infer it based on the assigned initializer. The syntax follows one of the following patterns:

```
var x int = 10
var y = 20
var z int
```

In the first declaration, x is explicitly typed as `int` and initialized to 10. In the second, the compiler infers the type of y as `int` because 20 is an integer literal; explicit type annotation is optional. The third declaration creates a variable z with type `int` but leaves it uninitialized; variables declared without explicit initializers are given the zero value of their type (0 for `int`, `""` for `string`, and so on).

`var` declarations can also span multiple variables simultaneously, allowing grouped declarations that enhance organizational clarity:

```
var (
    a int     = 1
    b string  = "hello"
    c float64
)
```

Here, c is declared without an initializer, so it is assigned the zero value `0.0`. Grouping declarations neatly packages related variables with clearly defined types and initial values, improving code readability.

Beyond `var`, Go introduces a concise short variable declaration form using `:=`. This shorthand automatically both declares the variable and initializes it with the value on the right-hand side. It requires type inference and is restricted to function-local scope:

```
func example() {
    count := 10
    name := "GoLang"
    active := true
}
```

The short declaration favors brevity and rapid development within function bodies. However, it cannot be used for package-level variables since the Go compiler demands explicit var declarations in that context for clarity and deterministic initialization ordering. Additionally, := requires at least one new variable on the left side; attempting to re-declare entirely existing variables results in compilation errors, encouraging a disciplined approach.

Variable scope and lifetime are tightly coupled with the declaration method. Variables declared with var at the package level reside in static memory, accessible throughout the package and initialized once at program start. In contrast, those declared using var or short declaration inside functions have block scope and automatic storage duration, allocated each time control enters the block.

Constants in Go are declared using the const keyword. Constants are immutable values known at compile time and can be of simple types such as booleans, numeric types, and strings. Their declaration resembles variable declarations but with distinct semantics:

```
const Pi = 3.14159
const Greeting string = "Hello, World!"
const (
    Zero  = 0
    One   = 1
    Two   = 2
)
```

Constants must be initialized with compile-time evaluable expressions-no run-time assignments or variables are allowed on the right-hand side. This restriction enables aggressive compiler optimizations, such as replacing constants with their literal values inline, thus improving performance and enabling better code analysis.

Constant declarations support the use of iota, a predeclared identifier which simplifies defining enumerated constants:

```
const (
    Red = iota
    Green
```

```
    Blue
)
```

In this snippet, Red is 0, Green is 1, and Blue is 2, automatically incremented by iota. This pattern minimizes redundant code and improves maintainability.

Initialization requirements differ markedly between variables and constants. Variables may be declared without explicit initializers, automatically acquiring a zero value, whereas constants require explicit initialization at declaration, reflecting their immutable and compile-time constant nature. Failing to initialize a constant results in a compilation error.

The choice between var, short declaration, or const impacts code readability and performance:

- var declarations with explicit types yield self-documenting code, especially useful for package-level variables and complex data types where clarity outweighs brevity.

- The short declaration (:=) is syntactically succinct, ideal for local variables where the type is evident from the right-hand side, thereby reducing boilerplate and enhancing focus on logic.

- Constants enable clear expression of fixed values contributing to domain invariants and allow the compiler to optimize away redundant computations.

Performance-wise, variables declared at package scope with var reside in static memory, eliminating repeated allocation overhead during function calls. Local variables with short declaration or var inside functions incur allocations on the stack, often invisible to the programmer but critical for memory management. Constants, being inlined by the compiler, impose no run-time memory overhead.

From a style and maintainability perspective, explicit var declarations aid large teams by making the codebase explicit about types and initialization, whereas the short declaration sharpens code conciseness and reduces verbosity in local contexts. Constants enhance program correctness by embedding fixed domain knowledge, reducing magic numbers and improving semantic clarity.

Go's trio of declaration styles-var, short declaration, and const-complement one another. The deliberate application of each, with an understanding of their initialization rules, scope implications, and performance characteristics, assists in crafting idiomatic, efficient, and maintainable Go programs.

3.2. Type Declarations and Aliasing

Go provides a flexible and expressive type system that supports creating new types and type aliases, each serving distinct purposes in structuring code and managing complexity. Understanding how to properly leverage type declarations and aliasing is vital for designing robust, maintainable APIs and ensuring clear type identity within Go programs.

At its core, type declarations in Go define a new named type based on an existing one. This form of declaration creates a completely new type, even if it shares the underlying structure with another. The syntax follows:

```
type NewType ExistingType
```

Here, NewType is a distinct type with the same underlying representation as ExistingType, but it is treated as incompatible with ExistingType by the compiler unless explicit conversion is performed. For instance,

```
type Celsius float64
type Fahrenheit float64
```

Although both are based on float64, assignments between variables of types `Celsius` and `Fahrenheit` are disallowed:

```
var tempC Celsius = 20.0
var tempF Fahrenheit = tempC // compile-time error: cannot use
    tempC (type Celsius) as type Fahrenheit in assignment
```

This strict separation enforces stronger type safety, enabling developers to encode domain semantics directly into the type system, reducing bugs associated with misuse of interchangeable primitive values.

Beyond declaring entirely new types, Go also offers *type aliases*, introduced in Go 1.9, which provide a way to define an alternate name for an existing type. The syntax employs the equals sign:

```
type Alias = ExistingType
```

Unlike a new type declaration, aliases share the exact same identity as the original type. They do not introduce a new, distinct type but rather create an interchangeable synonym. This is especially useful for code refactoring and maintaining backward compatibility without breaking existing clients.

Consider the alias declaration:

```
type MyInt = int
```

Here, `MyInt` is identical to `int` in every aspect-assignments, method sets, and interface compatibility are fully interchangeable. Aliasing is fundamentally about *name management* rather than type distinction.

Understanding when to employ new type declarations versus type aliases is crucial for API design and code clarity. New types are preferred to encapsulate domain-specific semantics and enforce invariants by leveraging Go's strict type checking. For instance, wrapping a `string` as a type `Email` helps document intent and prevent accidental misuse:

```
type Email string

func (e Email) IsValid() bool {
```

```
    // implementation omitted
    return true
}
```

The Email type can then have associated methods, and variables of type Email cannot be implicitly mixed with ordinary string values, reducing potential errors.

On the other hand, type aliases are valuable when renaming or re-organizing packages and types without disrupting client code that depends on existing type identities. For example, if a package restructures internal types but wants to expose the original type names for compatibility, aliases help maintain the contract:

```
// package oldpkg
type Data struct {...}

// package newpkg, internally moved
type dataInternal struct{...}
type Data = dataInternal  // alias to maintain API compatibility
```

Alias declarations influence Go's type identity profoundly. While new types differ from their bases in method sets and assignability, aliases share identical sets. Method receivers defined on the original type immediately apply to aliases, preserving behavior seamlessly. Conversely, new types must explicitly embed or redefine methods.

Aliasing does not support extending or modifying underlying types; it merely creates a new name. New type declarations enable extending behavior by attaching methods, yet require conversions to interact with the original base type or other new types sharing the same underlying structure.

In type checking and interface satisfaction, new types with distinct names do not automatically satisfy interfaces implemented by their underlying types; methods must be explicitly added. Aliases, however, satisfy exactly the same interfaces as the aliased type. This distinction informs design decisions concerning polymorphism and abstraction boundaries within APIs.

A delicate balance arises in designing APIs with Go's type system: employing new types increases type safety and code self-documentation, while excessive fragmentation may lead to cumbersome conversions and verbosity. Meanwhile, aliasing preserves seamless interoperability at the expense of semantic clarity.

Code reuse benefits from both mechanisms strategically. New types promote encapsulation and domain modeling, avoiding accidental interchangeability. Aliases facilitate evolution and refactoring without breaking external clients. Careful use of both enhances maintainability, readability, and robust interface design.

Go's dual approach to type declaration and aliasing offers complementary tools: new types introduce distinct identities aiding semantic clarity and safety, whereas aliases enable flexible naming and backward compatibility. Mastery of these features empowers developers to craft APIs that are both rigorously typed and evolvable, embodying idiomatic Go design principles.

3.3. Identifier Scope and Linkage

In the Go programming language, understanding the rules governing the scope and linkage of identifiers is fundamental to managing visibility, lifetime, and accessibility of variables, functions, constants, and types. Go employs a lexical scoping model combined with specific linkage conventions that control how identifiers are resolved within nested blocks, functions, and packages, as well as across compilation units.

Go's lexical scoping means that the location of an identifier's declaration within the source code dictates its visibility and lifetime. The compiler resolves identifier references based on the textual structure of the program, organized into nested blocks. These blocks may be files, packages, functions, or explicitly delimited code segments such as loops and conditionals.

Identifiers declared inside a block are visible from the point of declaration to the end of that block, including any nested inner blocks, but they are not accessible from outer or unrelated blocks. This containment ensures that inner declarations shadow outer ones with identical names.

Consider the following example illustrating nested block scope:

```go
package main

import "fmt"

func main() {
    x := 10            // 'x' visible from here to end of main
    {
        x := 20        // new scope, shadows outer 'x'
        fmt.Println(x) // prints 20
    }
    fmt.Println(x)     // prints 10 - outer 'x'
}
```

Here, the inner declaration of variable x shadows the outer x only within the inner block. Once outside, the outer variable regains visibility.

Within functions, identifiers have lifetimes tied to function invocation. All variables, constants, and types declared inside the body of a function exist only during the function's execution. Each subsequent call creates new instances of these identifiers.

Function parameters are considered local identifiers scoped to the function body, replacing any outer declarations with the same name. Likewise, variables declared with var or short variable declaration (:=) have block-level scope within the function.

Closures can capture variables from surrounding lexical scopes. This capability requires the Go runtime to allocate such variables on the heap rather than the stack to preserve their state after the enclosing function returns.

```go
func counter() func() int {
    count := 0
    return func() int {
        count++
```

61

```
        return count
    }
}
```

Here, the anonymous function refers lexically to count defined in the outer counter function scope. The variable count remains accessible each time the closure is invoked, demonstrating lifetime extension via captured lexical scope.

At the package level, declarations such as constants, variables, types, and functions are visible throughout the package. A package serves as the primary unit of encapsulation and namespace in Go, grouping related code together.

Identifiers declared at package scope but not exported (named with lowercase initial letters) are accessible only within the same package; they are invisible to other packages. Conversely, exported identifiers have uppercase initial letters, granting visibility and accessibility across package boundaries.

For example:

```
// package mathutil
package mathutil

// Exported function visible outside the package
func Add(a, b int) int {
    return a + b
}

// unexported variable - private to package
var internalCounter int
```

In another package, only Add can be accessed:

```
package main

import "mathutil"

func main() {
    sum := mathutil.Add(4, 5)  // permitted
    // mathutil.internalCounter // compilation error: undefined
}
```

This visibility model enforces modularity and information hiding by controlling access based on identifier naming conventions and package boundaries.

Within packages and functions, explicit block scopes are created using braces {}, such as within if, for, and switch statements. Any variables declared in these blocks shadow outer identifiers and cease to exist after the block terminates.

```
func example() {
    x := 1
    if true {
        x := 2    // shadows outer 'x' in this block only
        fmt.Println(x)
    }
    fmt.Println(x)
}
```

This defined scoping enables safer reuse of identifiers and reduces unintended side-effects across code segments.

Linkage determines the accessibility of identifiers across multiple source files and packages. Go's compilation unit is the package rather than individual source files. All Go source files with the same package clause are compiled together into a single package binary, sharing the same package scope.

Identifiers that are exported (starting with uppercase letters) have external linkage; they can be referred to from other packages after importing. Non-exported identifiers have internal linkage confined to the package.

The Go linker resolves references between packages using these linkage properties, enabling separate compilation while maintaining clear boundaries. Unlike languages such as C or C++, Go does not have separate declarations or header files because package-scoped declarations serve as the interface.

- **Block scope**: Identifiers are visible from the point of declaration to the end of the block.

- **Shadowing**: Inner declarations with the same name hide

outer ones within inner scope.

- **Function scope**: Locals exist per invocation, and parameters behave as local variables.

- **Closure captures**: Enclosed lexical variables may have extended lifetime.

- **Package scope**: Unexported identifiers are package-private; exported identifiers are accessible externally.

- **Linkage**: Exported identifiers have external linkage across compilation units; non-exported have internal linkage.

Proper understanding and utilization of Go's scoping and linkage mechanisms enable the construction of modular, maintainable, and encapsulated software systems, with controlled symbol visibility that supports concurrent development and team collaboration.

3.4. Package Structure and Imports

In Go, the organization of source code into packages forms the cornerstone of modular design, encapsulation, and dependency management. A package is a collection of related Go source files that share a common namespace. This section elucidates the syntax for package declarations, the semantics of import paths, the initialization order of packages, and pragmatic strategies to manage dependencies with an emphasis on avoiding circular imports.

Go source files begin by declaring the package to which they belong. The declaration syntax follows the form:

```
package packageName
```

Each source file in a directory must declare the same package name. By convention, package names are short, lowercase, and indicative of their functionality. For example, a directory containing utility

64

functions for HTTP operations might use package `httputil`. The package name determines the namespace visible to other packages and controls the scope of exported identifiers. Identifiers are exported only if they begin with an uppercase letter; otherwise, they remain unexported and thus private to the package.

The import mechanism in Go relies on import paths, which uniquely identify the desired package based on its location within the workspace or module repository. An import statement takes the form:

```
import "import/path"
```

Multiple packages can be imported within a single block:

```
import (
    "fmt"
    "net/http"
    "example.com/project/pkg/util"
)
```

Here, `"fmt"` and `"net/http"` are standard library packages, while the latter is a third-party or project-local package. The import path uses forward slashes regardless of the underlying filesystem. When using Go modules, the import path aligns with the module path plus the relative directory of the package, ensuring reproducible dependency resolution.

The package initialization process is rigorously defined to guarantee deterministic behavior. Each package may contain one or more `init()` functions, which perform setup tasks initialized before any other package code executes. The initialization order proceeds as follows:

1. For each package, the dependencies, identified via imports, are recursively initialized first.

2. Within a single package, all package-level variable declarations are evaluated in the order they appear in source files, respecting file compilation order.

3. Subsequently, `init()` functions are invoked in the textual order across the source files.

The Go runtime ensures that cyclic initialization dependencies do not cause deadlock by disallowing circular import cycles at compile time. Circular imports arise when two or more packages import each other directly or indirectly, leading to tangled dependencies and compilation errors.

To avoid circular imports, several strategies are commonly adopted:

- Refactoring into smaller packages: extract shared interfaces or utility functions into an independent package that both original packages can import. This decouples the dependency graph.

- Using interface abstractions: define interfaces in one package and implement them in another, breaking direct import dependencies.

- Dependency injection: pass dependencies as function parameters or struct fields rather than importing them directly, reducing coupling.

- Restructuring package responsibilities: reevaluate package boundaries to ensure clear separation of concerns.

To illustrate, consider two packages pkgA and pkgB. If pkgA imports pkgB and vice versa, the compiler raises an error:

```
import cycle not allowed
package pkgA
imports pkgB
imports pkgA
```

Refactoring might consist of creating a third package, pkgCommon, that holds shared types or interfaces:

```
// pkgcommon/interfaces.go
package pkgcommon

type Service interface {
    PerformTask() error
}
```

Then, pkgA and pkgB each import pkgcommon, eliminating the cycle:

```
// pkgA/some.go
package pkgA

import "example.com/project/pkgcommon"
```

Regarding import aliases, Go allows renaming imports to resolve naming collisions or improve readability. This is performed as:

```
import alias "import/path"
```

For instance,

```
import jsonenc "encoding/json"
```

enables referencing the package via jsonenc rather than json. Blank identifier imports import a package solely for its side-effects, triggering init() without binding any identifiers:

```
import _ "example.com/project/pkg/plugin"
```

The Go tooling promotes explicit and minimal imports, enhancing compile times and program clarity. Unused imports lead to compilation errors, incentivizing developers to keep dependencies lean.

Furthermore, the go mod system manages external dependencies, ensuring versioning, retrieval, and reproducibility of imported packages from remote repositories. This module-aware import resolution supersedes the older GOPATH mode, enforcing semantic import paths and eliminating ambiguity.

Package structuring and imports in Go revolve around clear package declarations, well-defined import paths, deterministic initialization order, and disciplined dependency management. Navigating complexities such as circular dependencies demands architectural foresight and techniques like modularization and interface abstraction. Mastery of these facets facilitates scalable, maintainable, and idiomatic Go programs.

3.5. Blank Identifier and Discards

The blank identifier, denoted by the underscore _, is a distinctive feature in several programming languages-most notably in Go-that serves as a versatile tool for discarding values or avoiding explicit variable declarations. This section elucidates the multifaceted roles and idiomatic uses of the blank identifier, highlighting how it simplifies code, reduces errors, and enhances program clarity when handling unwanted or unused values.

Discarding Unwanted Values

In many function calls or composite expressions, multiple return values are common. Often, only a subset of these values is relevant, while the rest are either redundant or intentionally ignored. Rather than declaring unnecessary variables, the blank identifier permits discarding such values, signaling to the reader and compiler that these outputs are intentionally unused.

For example, consider a function that returns both a result and an error:

```
func compute() (int, error) {
    // function implementation
}

result, err := compute()
```

If the error is not required (discouraged in robust applications, but possible in exploratory or prototype code), the blank identifier facilitates assignment without clutter:

```
result, _ := compute()
```

This idiomatic approach prevents compiler warnings about unused variables and clearly indicates that the error return is deliberately ignored.

Suppressing Unused Variable Errors

Compilers frequently produce errors or warnings when variables are declared but not used, a behavior designed to catch potential bugs early. The blank identifier offers an elegant mechanism to satisfy the compiler's requirement without retaining unnecessary variables.

An illustrative case involves importing packages to register side effects-a practice common in extensible frameworks or plugins. When a package's functionalities are triggered solely by its init() functions, the import must occur, but the imported package is not referenced explicitly in the code. To avoid "imported and not used" errors, the blank identifier imports the package anonymously:

```
import _ "example.com/package/plugin"
```

This informs the compiler to invoke the package's init() function without binding the import to a named identifier. Such usage is prevalent in database drivers, cryptographic providers, and middleware libraries where side effects matter more than direct code references.

Idiomatic Patterns Employing the Blank Identifier

Beyond discarding values, the blank identifier integrates into numerous idiomatic constructs that improve code readability and prevent subtle defects.

- *Loop Variables When Value Is Unused*: When iterating over a collection but only the index or value is needed, the unused component can be replaced with _.

```
for _, value := range values {
    process(value)
}
```

69

```
for index, _ := range values {
    fmt.Println(index)
}
```

- *Multiple Assignment with Partial Interest*: Functions returning multiple outputs can have selective assignments combined with discards, clarifying intent while maintaining brevity:

```
_, err := os.Stat("file.txt")
if err != nil {
    fmt.Println("File does not exist.")
}
```

- *Interface Implementations*: Sometimes, developers may want to confirm that a type satisfies an interface at compile time without instantiating it. The blank identifier can be used to assign a zero value of the type to an interface variable solely for verification:

```
var _ io.Writer = (*MyType)(nil)
```

This ensures MyType implements io.Writer without generating any runtime overhead or storing a variable.

Avoiding Subtle Errors

The blank identifier's judicious use can preempt common programming mistakes:

- *Unintended Shadowing*: In multi-value return contexts, failing to discard unused values may introduce shadowed variables, leading to logical errors. Using _ makes variable scope explicit and simplifies debugging.

- *Preventing Unused Variable Complaints*: Especially in iterative development or stubbing, programmers may temporarily ignore certain return values. Employing the blank identifier maintains clean builds and prevents distractions from compiler diagnostics.

70

- *Semantic Clarity*: Using _ communicates intentional omission, which is preferable to silently ignoring a variable, thus improving code maintainability.

Summary of Practical Use Cases

Scenario	Description
Value Discarding	Ignore unwanted return values without introducing useless variables.
Unreferenced Imports	Import packages purely for side effects (e.g., initialization) with anonymous import.
Unused Loop Variables	Skip indices or values that do not contribute to loop operations, enhancing readability.
Interface Compliance	Assert type implementation of interfaces at compile time without runtime cost.
Compiler Hygiene	Avoid unused variable warnings and potential shadowing through explicit discards.

The blank identifier embodies a minimalist and powerful tool, weaving into idioms that reconcile code expressiveness with compiler constraints. Mastery of this construct reduces boilerplate, clarifies intent, and safeguards against common pitfalls in robust and idiomatic programming practice.

3.6. Initialization Order and Dependencies

Go employs a well-defined, deterministic initialization order that governs the evaluation and setup of package-level variables, constants, and the execution of package initialization functions. Understanding these rules is essential for constructing reliable applications and libraries that initialize predictably and maintain safe state transitions during startup.

Initialization begins once all package dependencies are resolved, following a transitive dependency graph formed by import relationships. For each package, Go processes three distinct phases: constant evaluation, variable initialization, and the execution of `init` functions. These phases occur in a strictly ordered manner, with each phase completing entirely in a dependency-aware sequence before progressing.

The initialization order of packages correlates directly with the directed acyclic graph of package dependencies. If package A imports package B, then B's initialization completes before A starts. This ensures A can safely reference B's exported variables and constants during its own initialization.

More precisely, Go performs a topological sort on the import graph to establish a linear initialization order with no cyclic dependencies. Cyclic imports are disallowed to prevent indeterminate initialization states. Consequently, packages are initialized in layers: leaf packages (those without imports) first, followed by their dependents, culminating in the main package.

Within each package, initialization proceeds in two distinct phases before any `init` functions run:

1. Constants are evaluated first. Unlike variables, constants are evaluated at compile time. As such, their dependencies must be acyclic within the constant declarations themselves. Constants can depend on other constants but cannot depend on variables or runtime state.

2. Variables are initialized next. Variables declared at package scope are initialized in the order they are presented in the source code. Variable initializers can depend only on previously initialized package-level constants, variables, and externally imported package-level objects guaranteed to be fully initialized due to package initialization order semantics.

This strict ordering ensures no variable initializer references a yet-uninitialized package variable, preventing undefined behavior or runtime panics caused by partially initialized state. The deterministic order also aids comprehension of startup behavior and simplifies debugging initialization issues.

Package-level variable initializers may include function calls, but such functions must not depend on variables that have yet to be initialized. This constraint is essential to avoid "init loop" problems where initialization order dependencies would be ill-defined. The compiler and runtime system rely on the dependency graph and source code order to enforce this.

For instance, consider the scenario:

```
var x = f()
var y = x + 1
```

Here, f() executes before y is initialized, guaranteeing x holds a valid value for y's initializer. Attempting to access y before x completes initialization would cause a compile-time error or runtime panic.

Once constants and variables are fully initialized, Go executes init functions within each package, preserving the overall dependency ordering of packages. Multiple init functions can be defined per package and per source file; their execution order within a package is the order of their appearance in the source files as dictated by the compiler.

An init function typically carries out essential logic that requires fully available initialized state, such as registering types, performing sanity checks, or initializing runtime configurations. Because init functions execute after all variable initializers, developers can safely reference any package-level variable or constant within them.

Ensuring safe, predictable startup behavior requires adherence to several best practices addressing dependency chains and initialization side effects:

- Avoid complex inter-package initialization logic. Design packages to minimize intricate dependencies or global state mutations during initialization. Favor explicit initialization

73

functions over side-effectful variable initializers.

- Limit usage of global variables with interdependencies. Where global state is necessary, clearly document initialization order assumptions and consider breaking initializers into simpler, linear steps.

- Use `init` functions conservatively. Overuse can obscure initialization order; prefer explicit setup calls when feasible.

- Prevent cyclic dependencies. Modularity and a clean package hierarchy reduce initialization complexity and ensure acyclic dependency graphs.

- Test initialization paths extensively. Unit tests, especially with dependency injection, can help verify predictable startup order and detect unintended side effects early.

In some applications, complex dependency chains arise from layered abstractions or plugin architectures. Go resolves these by faithfully following the topological order of package imports. However, developers must remain vigilant for indirect initialization cycles or implicit dependencies via variable initializers calling into other packages.

When faced with such complexity, one effective technique is to decompose initialization into multiple stages:

1. Minimal initialization: use variable initializers strictly for pure, side-effect-free computations.

2. Explicit setup functions: export functions that perform runtime-dependent or ordering-sensitive initialization, invoked explicitly by the main package or an orchestrating package after all dependencies are fully loaded.

3. Lazy initialization: delay some initialization until first use, leveraging synchronization primitives to ensure thread safety.

By shifting away from large-scale, implicit initialization in variable declarations or `init` functions, developers gain control over timing and sequencing, mitigating risks related to hidden dependencies.

For clarity, the core Go initialization rules can be distilled as follows:

- Package dependency order establishes a strict acyclic order for package initialization.

- Constants are evaluated before variables, at compile time, allowing only constant dependencies.

- Package-level variables are initialized in source code order, using previously initialized constants and variables.

- `init` functions run after all variables are initialized, in the order determined by the compiler within a package, and respecting package dependency order.

- Cyclic package dependencies are disallowed; cyclic variable initialization dependencies are detected and rejected.

- Function calls during variable initialization must not rely on variables not yet initialized.

Adhering to these principles enables construction of robust, well-structured Go programs with predictable startup ordering. Mastery of initialization order and dependency resolution forms a foundation for advanced Go development, critical when authoring reusable libraries and complex applications alike.

Chapter 4

Functions, Methods, and Closures

Step into the engine room of Go's expressiveness: functions. This chapter unveils how Go treats functions as first-class citizens, empowering concise logic, powerful abstractions, and safe concurrency. Explore the interplay of methods and closures, and discover the design philosophies that let Go blend simplicity with deep flexibility.

4.1. Function Declaration and Invocation

In Go, functions are fundamental building blocks that encapsulate reusable logic, supporting structured and modular code design. A function declaration specifies a block of code that can be invoked elsewhere in a program, potentially with inputs and outputs. The core syntax is concise yet expressive, allowing multiple parameters, named return values, and variadic arguments.

A typical function declaration begins with the `func` keyword, fol-

lowed by the function name, parameter list enclosed in parentheses, optional return type(s), and the function body enclosed in
braces. Parameters are specified as identifiers followed by their
type. When multiple parameters share the same type, Go allows
omitting repeated type annotations to enhance brevity.

```
func add(x int, y int) int {
    return x + y
}
```

Parameters x and y have type int, and the function returns an int.
Go supports multiple return values, a distinctive feature that facilitates returning composite results or error values without resorting
to complex data structures.

```
func divide(dividend, divisor int) (quotient int, remainder int)
    {
    quotient = dividend / divisor
    remainder = dividend % divisor
    return
}
```

Here, named return variables quotient and remainder are declared in the signature. The explicit return statement without arguments returns the current values of those variables. Functions
can also return unnamed values.

Go supports variadic functions-those accepting an arbitrary number of arguments of a specified type. Variadic parameters are declared by preceding the type with an ellipsis (...). Such parameters must be the last in the parameter list.

```
func sum(nums ...int) int {
    total := 0
    for _, n := range nums {
        total += n
    }
    return total
}
```

The variadic parameter nums behaves like a slice of int inside the
function. When calling such a function, a sequence of arguments
can be passed, or a slice can be expanded using the ellipsis syntax.

Function invocation involves evaluating the arguments, evaluating the function expression, and then transferring control to the called function with the evaluated arguments. This process requires space allocation on the stack frame to hold arguments, return addresses, and local variables.

Go employs pass-by-value semantics by default. On invocation, the actual arguments are copied into the function's stack frame as parameter values. For primitive types like integers and floats, this copy is straightforward. For more complex types like arrays or structs, copying may be more expensive, and pointers are used for efficiency and mutability.

```
func increment(x int) int {
    x = x + 1
    return x
}

func main() {
    a := 5
    b := increment(a)
    fmt.Println(a, b) // Output: 5 6
}
```

The original variable a remains unchanged after passing to increment, demonstrating pass-by-value behavior.

Pointer parameters enable functions to modify values outside their scope by passing the address of a variable rather than a copy of its value.

```
func incrementPtr(x *int) {
    *x = *x + 1
}

func main() {
    a := 5
    incrementPtr(&a)
    fmt.Println(a) // Output: 6
}
```

Variadic arguments complicate stack allocation slightly: the compiler packages the variable number of arguments into a slice header, which internally contains a pointer to the contiguous

79

memory region holding the argument values, the length, and capacity. The caller allocates the needed memory and passes a pointer to this slice to the callee.

Functions themselves are first-class citizens in Go. A function name represents a function value, which can be assigned, passed, and invoked dynamically. The function type signature emphasizes the relationship between parameters and return types.

Stack management during function calls is efficient due to Go's calling convention, which passes arguments in registers where possible, falling back to the stack as needed. The compiler organizes stack frames to ensure quick invocation and safe return, supporting features like defer, panic, and recover that manipulate the call stack.

Go also supports anonymous functions and closures-function literals defined inline that can capture variables from their surrounding lexical environment. These constructs adhere to the same calling and stack usage conventions, with the captured variables stored in the heap if shared beyond their defining scope.

```
func main() {
    factor := 2
    multiply := func(x int) int {
        return x * factor
    }
    fmt.Println(multiply(3)) // Output: 6
}
```

Go's function declaration syntax directly supports flexibility in how data flows through code, enabling single and multiple arguments, variadic input, and multiple return values with straightforward syntax. The mechanics of argument passing involve stack-based call frames and pass-by-value semantics, augmented with pointer usage where mutability or performance is critical. Understanding these details is essential for leveraging Go's power effectively in performance-sensitive applications.

4.2. Multiple Return Values and Named Returns

Go's ability to return multiple values from a single function is a distinctive feature that enhances expressiveness and practicality in a wide array of programming scenarios. This capability not only supports idiomatic error handling but also simplifies function signatures by reducing the need for auxiliary data structures. Unlike many languages that restrict functions to a single return value, Go permits returning any number of values simultaneously, thereby streamlining the design of APIs and internal abstractions.

The syntax for multiple return values consists of listing the types of the return values within parentheses following the function signature. Consider a function that divides two floating-point numbers and returns both the quotient and the remainder as floats:

```
func divmod(x, y float64) (float64, float64) {
    quotient := x / y
    remainder := float64(int(x) % int(y))
    return quotient, remainder
}
```

Invoking such a function allows unpacking the results directly into distinct variables:

```
q, r := divmod(10.5, 3.0)
```

This straightforward mechanism reduces boilerplate code and avoids enforcing a custom struct solely to encapsulate multiple outputs.

Named return parameters appear within the function signature as named variables along with their types. This feature enables the function to predeclare the return values, which can then be assigned within the function body and finally returned implicitly without explicit mention. For example:

```
func split(sum int) (x, y int) {
    x = sum * 4 / 9
    y = sum - x
```

81

```
    return
}
```

Here, x and y act both as local variables and as return values. The implicit return statement, without any explicit operands, returns the current values of x and y.

Named returns can increase readability and reduce errors in functions with multiple outputs, especially when the meaning of each returned value is not immediately obvious. By labeling return parameters, a function's signature serves as partial documentation, which benefits maintainability and comprehension.

In practical Go programming, named return values are most beneficial when they add clarity to the code or when the function's logic requires several return paths that modify these values before the final return. However, overuse can lead to obscured flow or confusion if the return variables are shadowed or redefined within the function.

A commonly accepted idiom is to avoid named returns for simple or short functions where the return variables add no additional semantic clarity. For example, when a function returns just two values, such as a result and an error, naming the return parameters is often redundant because their meaning is usually explicit from contextual conventions.

One of Go's most pervasive patterns involves using multiple return values to return a value alongside an error indicator. This approach encourages explicit error checking immediately after a function call and is considered more transparent than relying on exceptions or error codes embedded in complex return types.

For instance:

```
func readFile(path string) ([]byte, error) {
    data, err := ioutil.ReadFile(path)
    if err != nil {
        return nil, err
    }
```

```
      return data, nil
}
```

In this case, an explicit `error` return value is always paired with the primary return type—here a byte slice. Named return parameters could optionally be used but typically are unnecessary since the return types are self-explanatory. The structure:

```
func readFile(path string) (data []byte, err error) {
    data, err = ioutil.ReadFile(path)
    return
}
```

is technically equivalent but less common due to its lack of immediate visual clarity in simple functions.

While named returns can reduce code verbosity, explicit `return` statements with specific values enhance readability in more complex functions. Employing named returns extensively in complex functions risks "floating return values," where the returned variables are modified deep in the logic, making it harder to trace value assignments without inspecting the full function body.

Explicit returns improve maintainability by localizing the return values and clarifying the function's exit points. The guideline is to reserve named returns for cases where the names significantly aid understanding—such as large functions with multiple return paths or when documenting subtle semantics of returned values.

Consider a function that attempts to parse an integer from a string and report success:

```
func parseInt(s string) (result int, err error) {
    result, err = strconv.Atoi(s)
    if err != nil {
        return 0, err
    }
    return result, nil
}
```

Here, although `result` and `err` are named in the signature, explicit return values are usually preferred to avoid confusion:

```
func parseInt(s string) (int, error) {
    result, err := strconv.Atoi(s)
    if err != nil {
        return 0, err
    }
    return result, nil
}
```

This form is more direct, clearly indicating the values returned at each exit point and minimizing any ambiguity regarding variable state throughout the function.

- Use multiple return values to express natural function outputs without packaging them into structs or arrays unnecessarily.

- Leverage named return parameters to improve code clarity when return values are complex or when multiple return points benefit from shared variable scope.

- Avoid named returns in small, straightforward functions to maintain explicitness and minimize cognitive load.

- Prioritize explicit `return` statements in functions with complex control flow to facilitate easier static analysis and debugging.

- Follow established idioms for error handling, returning a main value and an `error` value on all functions that may fail.

The balanced application of these principles results in Go programs that are both expressive and maintainable, effectively harnessing the power of multiple return values and named results without sacrificing clarity.

4.3. First-Class and Higher-Order Functions

In Go, functions are treated as first-class citizens, enabling them to be passed as arguments, returned from other functions, and assigned to variables. This feature profoundly affects expressive power and code modularity, facilitating flexible abstractions and the adoption of functional programming patterns. The ability to construct functions on the fly using function literals (anonymous functions) and to harness closures enables developers to encapsulate behavior, manage state, and build composable APIs in an elegant and concise manner.

Functions in Go have types that describe their parameter and return types, and these function types can be used as any other types. This capacity allows assigning functions to variables, storing them in data structures, or passing them as arguments. Consider the following example:

```
func add(a, b int) int {
    return a + b
}

var op func(int, int) int = add

result := op(3, 4) // result == 7
```

Here, the function `add` is assigned to the variable `op` of type `func(int, int) int`, illustrating that functions can be manipulated as runtime values. This ability opens the door to abstracting control flow and behavior by making functions parameters or return values, which is fundamental in higher-order programming.

Go supports defining functions anonymously at the point of use, often called function literals. These anonymous functions can be immediately invoked, stored, or passed along. Defining function literals reduces boilerplate when defining small, one-off behavior and is useful for callbacks, goroutines, or deferred execution contexts.

```
increment := func(x int) int {
```

```
        return x + 1
}

fmt.Println(increment(5)) // Output: 6
```

This function literal is assigned to the variable `increment` and invoked later, benefiting from lexical scoping of the surrounding environment. Anonymous functions can also be invoked directly:

```
result := func(a, b int) int { return a * b }(3, 7)
// result == 21
```

Constructing functions dynamically and invoking them inline promotes succinctness in cases where defining a named function would be unwieldy.

Closures arise when function literals capture variables from their lexical environment. These captured variables remain accessible even after the outer function has returned, enabling stateful behavior without the need for explicit structs or global variables.

```
func makeCounter() func() int {
    count := 0
    return func() int {
        count++
        return count
    }
}

counter := makeCounter()
fmt.Println(counter()) // 1
fmt.Println(counter()) // 2
```

In this example, the function returned by `makeCounter` closes over the variable `count`. Each invocation of `counter` increments and returns an internal state unique to that closure. Multiple closures created by repeated calls to `makeCounter` maintain independent states, illustrating the encapsulation capabilities enabled by closures.

It is essential to understand that closures capture variables by reference rather than by value. This can result in unintended shared state if loop variables or other mutable variables are captured improperly. For example, a common pitfall occurs in range loops:

```
func createFuncs() []func() int {
    funcs := []func() int{}
    for i := 0; i < 3; i++ {
        funcs = append(funcs, func() int {
            return i
        })
    }
    return funcs
}

funcs := createFuncs()
for _, f := range funcs {
    fmt.Println(f()) // Prints 3, 3, 3 instead of 0, 1, 2
}
```

The variable i is shared across closures, and by the time the functions run, i has reached the value 3. To fix this, an additional variable must be introduced inside the loop scope:

```
for i := 0; i < 3; i++ {
    i := i // shadowing within loop body
    funcs = append(funcs, func() int {
        return i
    })
}
```

This technique ensures that each closure captures a distinct copy of the loop variable.

A higher-order function is one that takes one or more functions as arguments or returns a function as its result. Go employs higher-order functions to enable elegant abstractions such as function composition, decorators, and predicates.

For example, a simple function that applies a given function to elements of a slice can be defined as:

```
func mapInts(input []int, fn func(int) int) []int {
    output := make([]int, len(input))
    for i, v := range input {
        output[i] = fn(v)
    }
    return output
}

squares := mapInts([]int{1, 2, 3}, func(x int) int { return x * x
```

```
    })
// squares == []int{1, 4, 9}
```

This common functional pattern abstracts the transformation operation over a collection, deferring the exact behavior to the passed function. The same principle extends naturally to filters, reducers, and other higher-level abstractions.

Functions returning functions are equally powerful. Consider a function that generates comparison predicates parameterized by a captured threshold:

```
func greaterThan(threshold int) func(int) bool {
    return func(x int) bool {
        return x > threshold
    }
}

gt10 := greaterThan(10)
fmt.Println(gt10(5))  // false
fmt.Println(gt10(15)) // true
```

This pattern encapsulates configuration within a generated function, facilitating modular and reusable conditional logic.

The combination of first-class functions, function literals, closures, and higher-order functions enables various powerful design patterns that improve expressiveness:

- **Callbacks and Event Handlers:** Functions passed as arguments to handle asynchronous or event-driven behavior.

- **Decorators and Middleware:** Functions wrapping others to modify behavior, common in HTTP handlers or logging layers.

- **Stateful Iterators and Generators:** Closures maintaining iteration state, controlling how values are produced on the fly.

- **Function Transformers:** Higher-order functions that compose or combine behaviors dynamically.

An example of a simple middleware function that wraps an HTTP handler by logging entry and exit times:

```
func loggingMiddleware(next func(w http.ResponseWriter, r *http.
    Request)) func(http.ResponseWriter, *http.Request) {
    return func(w http.ResponseWriter, r *http.Request) {
        start := time.Now()
        fmt.Println("Started:", r.URL.Path)
        next(w, r)
        fmt.Println("Completed in", time.Since(start))
    }
}
```

This demonstrates the natural synergy of higher-order functions and closures in building layered abstractions.

- **Function Types:** Functions have distinct types applicable wherever values of those types are required.

- **Anonymous Functions:** Enable inline, ephemeral function creation without explicit naming.

- **Closures:** Capture and retain access to lexical variables, facilitating encapsulated state.

- **Higher-Order Functions:** Operate on or return other functions, enhancing composability and abstraction.

- **Lexical Scoping Nuances:** Attention to variable capture semantics avoids common pitfalls with loop variables.

By embracing first-class and higher-order functions, Go programmers can build expressive, modular, and maintainable codebases that leverage both imperative and functional programming styles effectively.

4.4. Method Sets and Receivers

In Go, methods associate behaviors with types, enabling abstraction and polymorphism. The relationship between methods and

89

types is nuanced by the distinction between value and pointer receivers, which significantly influences method sets and interface
satisfaction. Understanding these interactions is fundamental to
mastering Go's type system, encapsulation, and method call semantics.

A method in Go is defined with a receiver argument, indicating the
type to which the method is bound. If the receiver is a value type,
for example T, the method operates on a copy of the receiver. If
the receiver is a pointer type, *T, the method operates on the original instance, allowing mutation of the receiver's underlying value.
Consider the following method definitions associated with a struct
type T:

```
type T struct {
    field int
}

func (t T) ValueReceiverMethod() {
    // operates on a copy of T
}

func (t *T) PointerReceiverMethod() {
    // operates on the original T via pointer
    t.field = 10
}
```

This difference has implications both in terms of method behavior
and method sets. The *method set* of a type is the set of methods
that can be called using a receiver of that type. Method sets differ
depending on whether the receiver is a value or pointer.

For a type T, the method set includes all methods declared with
receiver type T. Methods declared with pointer receiver type *T are
not included in the method set of T. Conversely, for the pointer type
*T, the method set includes all methods declared with receiver T as
well as those declared with receiver *T. This asymmetry enables
pointers to invoke all methods of the underlying value type, while
values cannot invoke methods declared only on pointers.

Formally, the method sets are:

$$\begin{cases} \text{MethodSet}(T) = \{m \mid m \text{ declared with receiver } T\} \\ \text{MethodSet}(*T) = \{m \mid m \text{ declared with receiver } T \text{ or } *T\} \end{cases}$$

This distinction plays a central role in interface satisfaction. An interface specifies a set of methods that a type must implement to satisfy it. When assigning a value of concrete type to an interface variable, the compiler checks whether the method set of the concrete type includes all methods required by the interface.

If an interface demands a method with receiver *T, a variable of concrete type T cannot satisfy this interface because T's method set excludes pointer receiver methods. However, a variable of type *T can satisfy the interface as its method set includes pointer receiver methods.

The converse is that if an interface requires only value receiver methods, both T and *T implement the interface, since *T's method set contains all of T's methods.

```
type Reader interface {
    Read() error
}

func (t T) Read() error {
    // implementation
    return nil
}

var r Reader = T{}    // valid: 'Ts method set includes Read
var rp Reader = &T{} // valid: *T method set includes Read
```

If the method Read had a pointer receiver (t *T), then only variables of type *T would satisfy Reader.

The decision of whether to use value or pointer receivers in a method definition is guided not only by the need to mutate the receiver but also by considerations of method set behaviors and interface compatibility. Using pointer receivers generally allows methods to modify the receiver, avoids copying large structs, and extends the method set to allow both T and *T variables to invoke pointer receiver methods via implicit pointer indirection when the variable is addressable.

Implicit method calls through pointer indirection occur when a value receiver is addressable and a method with a pointer receiver is invoked; the compiler automatically takes the address of the value to call the pointer method. However, the reverse is not allowed; pointer types cannot call methods with value receivers unless explicitly dereferenced.

Encapsulation is also affected by method receivers and method sets. Methods with pointer receivers can modify unexported fields of the receiver, thereby controlling stateful mutations when only the pointer is exposed externally. Value receivers promote immutability by operating on copies, enabling safe method calls without side effects on the original instance. Consequently, interfaces designed to expose immutable behaviors tend to specify value receiver methods, while those requiring mutation specify pointer receiver methods.

In concurrent programming patterns, pointer receivers are often preferred to avoid costly copies of large types and to ensure shared state mutation is deliberate. Nevertheless, value receiver methods are idiomatic for small structs or when representing immutable values.

The interplay between method sets, pointer versus value receivers, and interface satisfaction is critical for designing robust abstractions. Choosing receiver types influences how types implement interfaces, how methods are called, and what guarantees method semantics provide regarding state mutation. By mastering these relationships, Go programmers can create clear and efficient APIs that leverage Go's type system strengths without surprising behaviors.

Ultimately, method sets serve as the bridge connecting type methods to interface contracts, with receivers controlling the accessibility and mutability landscape. This equilibrium between method semantics and type behaviors is at the core of Go's approach to encapsulation, composition, and polymorphism.

4.5. Defer, Panic, and Recover

Go's approach to flow control extends beyond conventional conditionals and loops to incorporate mechanisms for managing cleanup actions and exceptional conditions in a predictable and structured manner. The constructs defer, panic, and recover serve as essential tools for enhancing program robustness, providing means for guaranteed resource management and error resilience within a clear control flow.

The defer statement postpones the execution of a function call until the surrounding function returns, regardless of whether that return is normal or due to a panic. This scheduling ensures that cleanup or finalization steps-such as closing files, unlocking resources, or flushing buffers-always occur in a predictable sequence. Deferred function calls are pushed onto a stack specific to the current goroutine, meaning they execute in last-in, first-out (LIFO) order upon return.

For example, consider managing a file resource:

```
func processFile(filename string) error {
    file, err := os.Open(filename)
    if err != nil {
        return err
    }
    defer file.Close() // Guarantees file closure upon function
     return

    // Perform processing on the file
    // Any early return still triggers file.Close()
    return nil
}
```

If the processFile function encounters an error or returns early, `file.Close()` is still invoked, preventing resource leakage. Multiple `defer`s can be used, and their order of execution is critical to understand. For example:

```
func example() {
    defer fmt.Println("First")
    defer fmt.Println("Second")
    fmt.Println("Doing work")
}
```

This will print:

```
Doing work
Second
First
```

as the deferred calls execute in reverse order. This LIFO ordering allows nested resource management to be naturally expressed.

While `defer` caters to routine cleanup, Go's model for handling unexpected conditions takes inspiration from exception handling but with a more explicit and controlled design. The `panic` function halts the normal flow of control by stopping the current goroutine's execution and unwinding the stack, executing deferred calls along the way. This immediate transfer of control signals a severe runtime error that cannot be handled by returning an error normally.

`panic` usage typically signifies unrecoverable states such as index out-of-bounds, nil pointer dereference, or explicit runtime checks that cannot proceed safely. However, panics should not be overused for general error reporting-Go encourages returning error values for expected error scenarios to keep control flow clear and predictable.

Preventing the abrupt termination caused by a `panic` is possible using the `recover` function, which regains control within a deferred function and retrieves the value passed to `panic`. If `recover` is called outside of a deferred function or when no panic is active, it returns `nil`. This behavior allows selective handling or cleanup after a panic, enabling some containment of fatal errors without crashing the entire program.

An idiomatic pattern for combining defer, panic, and recover looks like this:

```
func safeExecute() {
    defer func() {
        if r := recover(); r != nil {
            fmt.Printf("Recovered from panic: %v\n", r)
            // Perform additional error handling or cleanup
        }
    }()

    // Code that may panic
    mightPanic()
    fmt.Println("Completed without panic")
}
```

Here, the anonymous deferred function checks for a panic using recover. If a panic occurred, it prints the panic value and prevents the program from crashing. This mechanism allows creating fault-tolerant modules that isolate failures and gracefully degrade or log errors.

The interplay between defer, panic, and recover can be further illustrated by understanding the stack unwinding process. When a panic is triggered:

- Execution halts at the panic point, and the runtime begins unwinding the call stack.

- Deferred functions on each stack frame are executed in LIFO order.

- If a recover call is encountered within a deferred function, it captures the panic, halting further unwinding.

- Control returns to the deferred function, and then normal flow resumes after the deferred function returns.

- If no recover is found, the program crashes and prints the panic value along with a stack trace.

This controlled stack unwinding ensures that cleanup code is always executed even in the presence of critical errors, and that panics can be contained when appropriate.

An important caveat is that `recover` can only regain control inside deferred functions; calling `recover` elsewhere in the call stack will have no effect. This explicit scoping encourages deliberate panic handling close to the failure context or at appropriate higher-level boundaries designed for fault containment.

Because deferred calls may themselves invoke panics, Go's nested defer handling must be considered carefully. If a deferred function panics while recovering from another panic, the program will terminate immediately, as double panics are not recoverable.

In practical applications, `defer` is extensively used to ensure resource safety without verbose manual cleanup. `panic` and `recover` provide a structured yet lightweight approach to error escalation and recovery, supporting the development of reliable and maintainable systems. Together, these flow-control constructs contribute significantly to Go's simplicity, efficient resource management, and robust error resilience.

4.6. Recursive Functions and Tail Call Considerations

In Go, recursion is a fundamental technique where a function calls itself directly or indirectly to solve problems by breaking them down into smaller subproblems. Each recursive invocation creates a new stack frame, holding parameters, local variables, and return addresses. Understanding the relationship between recursion and stack growth is essential for writing safe and efficient Go programs.

When a recursive function is invoked, the Go runtime allocates a new stack frame within the goroutine's stack. Unlike fixed-size stacks in some languages, Go uses segmented stacks that grow and shrink dynamically. Therefore, each goroutine starts with a small initial stack (typically 2 KB) which increases incrementally as deeper recursion demands more stack space. Although this design mitigates early stack overflow, excessively deep recursion may still lead to runtime stack overflow or increased overhead due to frequent stack copying and relocation.

An idiomatic recursive function in Go typically has a clear base case ensuring termination and a recursive case that moves toward this base case. Consider the classic example of computing factorial:

```go
func factorial(n int) int {
    if n <= 1 {
        return 1
    }
    return n * factorial(n-1)
}
```

This implementation directly translates the mathematical definition but causes a stack frame for each decrement of n. While suitable for moderate values, factorial computations for large n are better handled iteratively to avoid deep recursion.

Recursion is particularly effective for problems naturally expressed by divide-and-conquer strategies, such as tree traversals or combinatorial search. In Go, recursive functions enable elegant and concise expressions of algorithms like depth-first search:

```go
type Node struct {
    Value    int
    Children []*Node
}

func traverse(n *Node) {
    if n == nil {
        return
    }
    process(n.Value)
    for _, child := range n.Children {
        traverse(child)
    }
}
```

Here, `traverse` recursively explores each child node. Each call creates a distinct stack frame, but because the depth typically matches the tree height, the stack growth is naturally bounded.

Tail recursion is a special case where a recursive call is the last operation performed in a function. In some functional languages or compilers, such calls can be optimized to reuse the current function's stack frame instead of creating a new one, known as tail call optimization (TCO). TCO converts recursion into iteration under the hood, providing constant stack space usage for tail-recursive functions.

Unfortunately, Go does not currently implement tail call optimization. The Go compiler does not transform tail calls to iterative loops at the machine code level. As a result, even tail-recursive functions may incur stack growth proportional to recursion depth, potentially leading to stack overflow in extreme cases.

To illustrate, consider the tail-recursive version of a factorial function that uses an accumulator parameter:

```
func factorialTail(n, acc int) int {
    if n <= 1 {
        return acc
    }
    return factorialTail(n-1, n*acc)
}
```

Although `factorialTail` is tail-recursive, Go will create a new stack frame for each recursive call. This limitation discourages reliance on deep recursion in performance-critical or resource-constrained Go applications.

Consequently, idiomatic Go often favors explicit iteration over deep or unbounded recursion. When recursion is required due to problem structure, programmers should ensure recursion depth remains reasonable or convert tail-recursive functions into loops explicitly. For example, `factorialTail` can be refactored iteratively:

```
func factorialIter(n int) int {
```

```
    acc := 1
    for i := 1; i <= n; i++ {
        acc *= i
    }
    return acc
}
```

This iterative approach uses constant stack space and typically executes faster.

It is important to note that Go's runtime optimizes for arbitrary stack growth by growing goroutine stacks in small increments, but this overhead can be non-negligible in extremely deep recursion. Profiling and benchmarking recursive code in Go can reveal performance bottlenecks linked to excessive stack allocations or copying.

Recursion in Go provides a clear and expressive mechanism for solving suitable problems. However, Go's lack of tail call optimization necessitates careful consideration of recursion depth and stack implications. Developers are encouraged to write clear base cases, avoid unnecessary deep recursion, and prefer iteration or explicit stack management when feasible. Understanding these constraints ensures recursive code remains performant, maintainable, and robust within Go's runtime environment.

Chapter 5

Interfaces, Composition, and Reflection

Encounter the core of Go's agility: how interfaces and composition unlock expressive, modular programs without the baggage of inheritance. This chapter reveals how Go's type system encourages loose coupling, code reuse, and dynamic behavior— culminating in the advanced magic of reflection for runtime introspection and adaptability.

5.1. Interface Declaration and Satisfaction

In Go, interfaces serve as fundamental abstractions that enable flexible and extensible program design. Unlike many traditional object-oriented languages where interface implementation must be explicitly declared, Go embraces implicit implementation: any type that implements the required methods automatically satisfies the interface, without explicit syntax to declare this. This mechanism is central to Go's design philosophy of minimalism and composability.

An interface type in Go specifies a set of method signatures. It defines *what* behavior is required, not *how* it is implemented:

```
type Reader interface {
    Read(p []byte) (n int, err error)
}
```

Here, Reader is an interface with a single method Read. Any type that implements a method with this exact signature implicitly satisfies the Reader interface.

The critical point is that satisfaction of an interface in Go is *structural*, not nominal. This means there is no need to declare that a type implements an interface explicitly. The compiler determines interface satisfaction based solely on method sets. Hence, if a concrete type File has a method:

```
func (f *File) Read(p []byte) (n int, err error)
```

then *File satisfies the Reader interface. Note that pointer receivers vs. value receivers affect the method set and, consequently, interface satisfaction. A pointer receiver method is associated only with the pointer type, whereas methods with value receivers belong to both pointer and value types.

Interfaces can specify multiple methods:

```
type ReadWriter interface {
    Read(p []byte) (n int, err error)
    Write(p []byte) (n int, err error)
}
```

A type satisfies this interface only if it provides both Read and Write methods with identical signatures. This strict, signature-based requirement ensures precise adherence while allowing maximum flexibility.

This implicit satisfaction enables a powerful extensibility pattern.

Functions and data structures can operate on interfaces instead of concrete types, thus supporting polymorphism through behavior rather than inheritance hierarchies. For instance, a function that processes any Reader can accept a file, a network connection, a buffer, or any custom type implementing Read.

```
func process(r Reader) error {
    buf := make([]byte, 1024)
    n, err := r.Read(buf)
    if err != nil {
        return err
    }
    // process buf[:n]
    return nil
}
```

This decouples code from concrete implementations, adhering to the dependency inversion principle and promoting cohesion.

The structural typing also empowers composition. Types can embed other types or interfaces, and as long as the embedded types provide the requisite methods, the composing type will satisfy the interface automatically. For example,

```
type Buffer struct {
    data []byte
}

func (b *Buffer) Read(p []byte) (n int, err error) {
    // implementation
    return
}

func (b *Buffer) Write(p []byte) (n int, err error) {
    // implementation
    return
}

type ReadWriteBuffer struct {
    *Buffer
}
```

Here, ReadWriteBuffer automatically satisfies the ReadWriter interface by virtue of embedding *Buffer, which has the necessary methods.

Implicit satisfaction reduces coupling between interface definitions and implementing types, facilitating easier code evolution. Interfaces can be extended with new methods, but this requires careful coordination because adding methods breaks existing implementations that do not define the new methods. A common idiom in Go is to design small, focused interfaces with minimal methods to maximize reusability and minimize breakage-for example, the standard library's io.Reader and io.Writer each have a single method.

For comprehensive understanding, the method set of a type affects the interfaces it satisfies:

- A value type (e.g., T) method set includes methods with receiver type T.

- A pointer type (e.g., *T) method set includes methods with receiver type T and *T.

For example, if a method has a pointer receiver, the value type does not automatically satisfy the interface requiring that method, but the pointer type does.

Interface values in Go are represented as a tuple: a pair of the concrete value and the concrete type implementing the interface. This dual structure enables dynamic dispatch: method calls on interface variables are resolved at runtime to the underlying concrete type's method implementation, supporting polymorphic behavior without explicit virtual tables as in C++.

This design encourages abstraction by hiding implementation details behind interfaces. Clients of an interface know only about the methods defined by it, permitting changes to the underlying types without affecting code dependent on the interface, reinforcing encapsulation.

Finally, interfaces foster the idiomatic Go pattern of "duck typing" – if a type "quacks like a duck" by implementing the right methods, it is accepted as a duck without any explicit assertion. This flexibility, coupled with static typing, ensures both safety and adaptability.

Go's interface declaration and implicit satisfaction mechanism underpin decoupled and extensible software design, encouraging composition over inheritance and enabling powerful abstractions through minimal, reusable contracts defined purely by behavior.

5.2. Dynamic Dispatch and Type Assertions

When a value is assigned to an interface type, the language runtime encapsulates two critical pieces of information: a pointer to the concrete value and a pointer to a type descriptor that represents the methods the value implements. This internal structure forms what is commonly known as the interface value representation. It establishes a robust foundation for the implementation of dynamic dispatch-the capability to invoke methods on values whose exact types are not known until runtime.

More formally, an interface value can be modeled internally as a pair (type, data). Here, type is a reference to a method table (or *itab*) describing the concrete type of the value and the method implementations corresponding to the interface, while data is a pointer to the actual instance of the concrete value. The method table represents a contract linking interface method signatures to their specific implementations on the concrete type, required for dynamic dispatch to resolve method calls at runtime.

Consider a value of some concrete type T assigned to an interface variable I. The runtime builds an interface value where the type portion points to T's method set compatible with I, and the data portion is a pointer to the T value itself. Subsequent invocations of an interface method on I cause the runtime to consult the type pointer to locate the correct function pointer from the method table, then call that function with the data pointer as the receiver argument. This procedure allows uniform handling of method calls independent of the underlying concrete type.

The polymorphic dispatch mechanism crucially depends on the careful organization of the method tables for each concrete type that implements the interface. The runtime guarantees that all methods declared by the interface exist in the method table with stable offsets, providing direct indexing without the need for expensive name lookups or reflection during method invocation. This efficiency is essential for performance-sensitive applications that rely heavily on interfaces.

Dynamic dispatch inherently leads to a form of type erasure, hiding concrete-type information from callers working only with interface variables. To recover the concrete type information at runtime, type assertions and type switches are indispensable. These constructs allow programs to extract and manipulate the underlying concrete value safely and efficiently, even when initially accessed via an interface.

A *type assertion* uses the syntax:

```
value, ok := interfaceValue.(ConcreteType)
```

The operation tests whether the dynamic type stored inside the interface value matches ConcreteType. If the assertion succeeds, ok is set to true and value holds the concrete value corresponding to ConcreteType. If it fails, ok is false and value is the zero value of ConcreteType. This mechanism allows programs to distinguish safely between different dynamic types stored in the same interface.

Internally, the runtime compares the type pointer within the interface value against the type descriptor for ConcreteType. If they match, the data pointer is converted to the concrete type pointer and returned. This comparison is highly optimized due to the static type descriptors maintained by the runtime. Importantly, type assertions avoid reflection's overhead but still enable conventional Go-style type interrogation.

For cases requiring handling multiple possible concrete types, the *type switch* construct is used:

```
switch v := interfaceValue.(type) {
case ConcreteType1:
    // Handle v as ConcreteType1
case ConcreteType2:
    // Handle v as ConcreteType2
default:
    // Handle unknown types
}
```

The type switch internally performs sequential type assertions against each specified case clause. Upon a successful match, execution jumps to the corresponding case block with the concrete value bound to v. If no match occurs, the default branch is executed. Type switches offer clear and concise syntax to dispatch behavior based on the runtime type while maintaining type safety without redundant reflection calls.

In the presence of nested interfaces or interface values containing pointers to other interfaces, the runtime ensures that the interface pair representation remains consistently valid. Methods accessed through layers of interface embedding continue to use dynamic dispatch through the method tables relevant to the final concrete type.

It is also critical to recognize that method calls through interfaces always use pointers to values stored inside the interface (or the interface stores pointers to values). Therefore, changes made through interface-valued receivers can affect the original underlying data if they are pointer receivers, highlighting the importance of understanding value semantics versus pointer semantics when working with interfaces.

The ability to recover a value's concrete type and operate on it using type assertions and switches preserves the flexibility and extensibility of interface-based designs, while carefully balancing runtime efficiency and type safety. This combination enables powerful polymorphic abstractions without sacrificing performance or requiring explicit type casting typical in other programming languages.

To summarize, storing a value in an interface results in a compact runtime representation linking methods and data pointers, which facilitates dynamic dispatch through method tables. Type assertions and type switches unlock the concrete type information embedded in interfaces, enabling statically typed, safe extraction and handling of these types at runtime. This intricate interplay between interface representation, method dispatch, and type introspection forms a cornerstone of modern polymorphism in statically typed languages with rich interface semantics.

5.3. Interface Embedding and Composition

Interface embedding is a powerful design technique that enables the construction of more complex abstractions through the combination of smaller, focused interfaces. This approach fosters scalable API design by promoting modularity, reusability, and enhanced testability.

At its core, interface embedding allows one interface to incorporate the methods of another, effectively inheriting its contract and extending it with additional behavior. This composition paradigm contrasts with inheritance in object-oriented programming by favoring explicit composition over rigid hierarchies. Consider an example in the context of a data storage system, where distinct interfaces define discrete capabilities:

```
type Reader interface {
    Read(p []byte) (n int, err error)
}

type Writer interface {
    Write(p []byte) (n int, err error)
}

// Composite interface embedding Reader and Writer
```

```
type ReadWriter interface {
    Reader
    Writer
}
```

Here, ReadWriter composes the two smaller interfaces, Reader and Writer, implicitly requiring any implementation to satisfy both contracts. This pattern immediately yields several advantages:

- **Granularity and Flexibility:** The smaller interfaces represent minimal, orthogonal abstractions, allowing clients to depend precisely on the capabilities they require.

- **Incremental Building:** Complex interfaces emerge naturally by incrementally embedding simpler ones. This facilitates code reuse and reduces duplication.

- **Clear Intent:** Interface names succinctly communicate the set of behaviors guaranteed, improving readability and maintainability.

Beyond simple aggregation, interface embedding encourages the encapsulation of domain-specific behavior in small, single-responsibility interfaces. For example, a network service interface could embed multiple protocol or utility interfaces:

```
type Connecter interface {
    Connect(address string) error
}

type Disconnector interface {
    Disconnect() error
}

type Service interface {
    Connecter
    Disconnector
    Status() string
}
```

Such design enables implementations to evolve independently for each behavioral aspect and provides test doubles facilely tailored to subsets of functionality, crucial for unit testing. Mocking a `Connecter` without implementing `Disconnector` becomes straightforward, enhancing test isolation and speed.

Another salient point concerns API scalability through incremental interface extensions. As a system grows, new capabilities can be added by defining new small interfaces and composing them with existing ones, avoiding breaking changes or redundant method declarations:

```
type Logger interface {
    Log(message string)
}

type AdvancedLogger interface {
    Logger
    LogError(err error)
}
```

Client code depending on `Logger` remains unaffected by the introduction of `AdvancedLogger`, which extends the interface with error-specific logging functionality. This approach aligns with the interface segregation principle, advocating for fine-grained interfaces to minimize client coupling.

When interfacing with third-party libraries or legacy code, embedding facilitates adapter patterns. By embedding a smaller interface corresponding to the external contract, developers can compose local abstractions that internalize external dependencies cleanly, improving maintainability:

```
type ExternalDBInterface interface {
    Query(query string) (Result, error)
}

type DB interface {
    ExternalDBInterface
    BeginTransaction() error
}
```

In this example, DB adapts an external interface while adding local extensions. This compositional pattern allows incremental migration or enhancement without monolithic rewrites.

Embedding also benefits from language-level support for interface satisfaction inference. In statically typed languages with structural typing, such as Go, embedding interfaces ensures that any type implementing the embedded interfaces automatically implements the composite one. This significantly reduces boilerplate and improves clarity without explicit declaration.

However, care must be taken to avoid overly large aggregated interfaces, which may lead to "fat interfaces" that are harder to implement and test. When an interface grows too large, it often signals the need to refactor and decompose responsibilities into smaller, more cohesive interfaces. Intrinsic to this decomposition is the recursive application of interface embedding, allowing a tree-like or layered interface hierarchy.

Interface embedding and composition promote the design of robust, composable contracts. These contracts serve as foundational abstractions in scalable APIs, balancing granularity and expressiveness, enhancing code reuse, facilitating testing, and enabling evolutionary growth without impact on existing clients. The resulting abstractions lead to well-structured codebases that adapt gracefully to complexity over time.

5.4. Reflect Package and Type Information

The Go programming language provides the `reflect` package as a powerful tool to inspect and manipulate objects at runtime, leveraging their type information. Reflection facilitates dynamic operations that are otherwise impossible or cumbersome with static typing alone. By accessing the metadata of types, values, and their interfaces, developers can write flexible functions and frameworks that adapt to input types during execution. The cornerstone of reflection in Go revolves around the `reflect.Type` and `reflect.Value` types, representing the static and dynamic views of Go objects respectively.

At the core, reflect.Type conveys the complete description of a type. It can be obtained from a value using:

```
var x interface{} = 42
t := reflect.TypeOf(x)
```

Here, t holds information about the concrete type of x, in this case int. This Type provides methods to query properties such as the name of the type (Name()), its package path (PkgPath()), whether it is an interface (Kind() == reflect.Interface), and its composite structure in the case of arrays, structs, slices, and so forth. For instance, a struct type can be analyzed field-by-field using NumField() and Field(i), demonstrating the reflection package's introspective capabilities.

Complementing reflect.Type is reflect.Value, which encapsulates the actual runtime value of a variable. ValueOf retrieves this metadata:

```
v := reflect.ValueOf(x)
```

The reflect.Value object provides methods to access the underlying data, convert it, and update it when possible. Importantly, Value represents the run-time storage, and if it is settable, one can modify it dynamically. For example, modifying the value requires an addressable Value, typically obtained from a pointer:

```
var y int = 10
v := reflect.ValueOf(&y).Elem()
v.SetInt(20)
fmt.Println(y) // Outputs: 20
```

In the example above, the pointer to y is passed to reflect.ValueOf, allowing Elem() to dereference it and obtain a modifiable Value. This approach illustrates essential reflection semantics: only addressable values can be modified via reflection.

Inspection of complex composite types such as structs and slices is straightforward. Consider a struct:

```
type Person struct {
```

```
        Name string
        Age  int
}

p := Person{"Alice", 30}
v := reflect.ValueOf(p)
t := v.Type()
```

One can iterate through the fields:

```
for i := 0; i < v.NumField(); i++ {
    field := v.Field(i)
    fmt.Printf("Field %d: %s = %v\n", i, t.Field(i).Name, field.
    Interface())
}
```

This outputs each field name alongside its value, extracted via `Interface()`, which returns the value as an `interface` suitable for type assertions or further handling.

Modifications of struct fields through reflection follow similar rules: only exported fields of addressable structs can be changed. Attempting to modify unexported fields or values derived from non-addressable values triggers runtime panics. When dynamic setting is needed, it is imperative to pass a pointer to the struct:

```
pv := reflect.ValueOf(&p).Elem()
nameField := pv.FieldByName("Name")
if nameField.IsValid() && nameField.CanSet() {
    nameField.SetString("Bob")
}
```

The function `CanSet()` ensures the field meets the criteria for modification. The `SetString()` method exemplifies a group of type-specific `Set` methods, including `SetInt`, `SetFloat`, and `SetBool`, each constrained by the field's underlying type.

Moreover, `reflect` exposes metadata useful for type-driven logic beyond simple value modification. For example, one can inspect method sets:

```
t := reflect.TypeOf(p)
for i := 0; i < t.NumMethod(); i++ {
    method := t.Method(i)
    fmt.Println("Method:", method.Name, "Type:", method.Type)
```

```
}
```

This iteration lists method names and their signatures available on the type.

Type assertions at runtime can be composed using reflection to dynamically invoke methods or validate interfaces. For instance, checking if a value implements a specific interface:

```
var readerType = reflect.TypeOf((*io.Reader)(nil)).Elem()

v := reflect.ValueOf(someObject)
if v.Type().Implements(readerType) {
    fmt.Println("someObject implements io.Reader")
}
```

Other advanced uses include dynamically creating new instances with `reflect.New()`, which returns an addressable `reflect.Value` initialized to the zero value of the specified type. This capacity allows factories or serialization engines to instantiate types unknown at compile time.

In addition, the reflect package facilitates examination of struct field tags, which are annotations used by many Go libraries for serialization, validation, and more. Consider:

```
type Config struct {
    Port int     `json:"port" default:"8080"`
    Host string `json:"host"`
}

cType := reflect.TypeOf(Config{})
portField, _ := cType.FieldByName("Port")
tag := portField.Tag.Get("default")
fmt.Println("Default Port:", tag)
```

Accessing field tags enables one to build sophisticated metadata-driven systems and leverage custom annotations encoded within Go source code.

Reflection is computationally expensive and bypasses certain static guarantees; therefore, it is generally recommended to use it judiciously, when flexibility truly outweighs complexity and performance costs. Still, its inclusion in Go empowers a broad range of dynamic patterns including object serialization, dependency injection, schema validation, and more.

The `reflect` package serves as the gateway to runtime type introspection and manipulation in Go. Through `reflect.Type` and `reflect.Value`, it grants fine-grained control over program data, enabling inspection, dynamic adaptation, and modification. Mastery of reflection unlocks considerable expressive power, allowing Go programs to transcend static limitations while maintaining type safety and idiomatic structure.

5.5. Empty Interface and Unstructured Data

In Go, the empty interface, denoted as `interface{}`, serves as a universal container capable of holding values of any type. This arises from Go's interface mechanism, where every type inherently implements the empty interface because it specifies zero methods. Consequently, `interface{}` functions as a fundamental building block for managing unstructured or dynamically-typed data, enabling the design of highly flexible APIs, generic data structures, and interaction with arbitrary payloads.

When a value of any type is assigned to a variable of type `interface{}`, the runtime representation is internally stored as a pair: the concrete type information and a pointer to the actual data value. This dual nature allows type assertions and type switches to recover the original concrete type when required. Consider the following example:

```
var v interface{}
v = 42          // assign an int value
v = "hello"     // reassign a string value
```

Here, v can hold any type of data dynamically. While this makes `interface{}` extremely versatile, it sacrifices compile-time type safety, demanding disciplined handling to avoid runtime errors.

Best Practices Using the Empty Interface

Effective utilization of the empty interface revolves around careful type management and explicit type recovery. Three key practices emerge:

- **Type Assertions:** To regain type safety after storing data in an empty interface, use the type assertion syntax:

```
val, ok := v.(int)
if ok {
    // val is now of type int
} else {
    // v does not hold an int
}
```

This pattern permits safe extraction of the original type, preventing panics caused by erroneous type conversions.

- **Type Switches:** When handling multiple potential types stored in an empty interface, type switches provide a clean, structured way to classify and process each type accordingly:

```
switch val := v.(type) {
case int:
    // handle int case
case string:
    // handle string case
default:
    // handle unknown type
}
```

This approach improves code readability and robustness, reducing runtime surprises.

- **Use in APIs and Data Structures:** Empty interfaces enable the creation of functions and data structures that operate on arbitrary data. For example, a logger function accepting any value:

```
func Log(v interface{}) {
    fmt.Printf("%#v\n", v)
}
```

While powerful, such flexibility requires disciplined documentation and cautious downstream type casting.

Pitfalls in Handling Unstructured Data

The flexibility of `interface{}` carries inherent risks primarily associated with deferred type errors and loss of type guarantees:

- **Unchecked Type Assertions:** Performing a type assertion without the comma-ok idiom may lead to a panic if the underlying type does not match:
  ```
  val := v.(int)    // panics if v does not hold an int
  ```
  Avoiding panics demands always using the two-value form to safely verify types.

- **Loss of Compile-Time Safety:** Storing values in `interface{}` effectively defers all type checking until runtime, negating compile-time guarantees and increasing the possibility of subtle bugs.

- **Ambiguous Semantics in Data Handling:** Overuse of empty interfaces, especially in deep call chains, can create "black box" code that is hard to analyze and maintain, since the actual expected types must be gleaned by inspection or documentation.

- **Performance Considerations:** Excessive use of empty interfaces may cause runtime overhead from boxing and unboxing values, and may inhibit compiler optimizations dependent on static type information.

Restoring Type Safety: Approaches and Patterns

To regain type safety and minimize the risks of unstructured data, the following techniques are commonly employed:

- **Use of Structs and Typed Wrappers:** Encapsulating unstructured data within well-defined structs rather than raw `interface{}` drastically improves type clarity:

117

```
type Event struct {
    Name    string
    Payload interface{}
}
```

Here, `Payload` can remain flexible, but the `Event` semantics are explicitly typed.

- **Encoding and Decoding to Known Types:** In scenarios involving JSON or other serialized formats, dynamically parsed data can be unmarshaled first into `map[string]interface{}` or `[]interface{}` to represent arbitrary structures. Subsequently, dedicated types and functions convert these into strongly typed Go structures.

- **Use of Reflection as Last Resort:** Reflection via the `reflect` package permits runtime type inspection and manipulation beyond what empty interfaces provide. However, reflection should be minimized because it complicates code and hampers static analysis.

- **Generics (Go 1.18+):** With the advent of generics in Go, many use cases for `interface{}` can now be replaced by parametric polymorphism, preserving type safety without sacrificing flexibility.

Example: Safely Handling JSON with Empty Interfaces

When decoding JSON of unknown or dynamic structure, the Go standard library typically uses `interface{}` to represent untyped data. The following example illustrates decoding into `interface{}`, then restoring typed access via assertions:

```
import (
    "encoding/json"
    "fmt"
)

func parseJSON(data []byte) {
    var v interface{}
    if err := json.Unmarshal(data, &v); err != nil {
```

```
        panic(err)
    }

    m, ok := v.(map[string]interface{})
    if !ok {
        fmt.Println("Expected a JSON object")
        return
    }

    if name, ok := m["name"].(string); ok {
        fmt.Println("Name:", name)
    } else {
        fmt.Println("Name field missing or not a string")
    }
}
```

```
Input JSON: {"name":"Gopher","age":5}
Output:
Name: Gopher
```

This pattern highlights the necessity of verifying each field's presence and type before use, illustrating how empty interfaces provide necessary indirection but require explicit type restoration.

Summary of Considerations

Harnessing the empty interface in Go unlocks potent capabilities for handling unstructured, dynamic, or heterogeneous data. Responsible design demands:

- Clear documentation of expected types when passing `interface{}` values.

- Rigorous use of type assertions and switches for type recovery, avoiding unchecked conversions.

- Favoring strongly typed abstractions and generics over pervasive empty interface usage.

- Awareness of performance implications and maintenance complexity.

Mastering these principles enables effective use of the empty interface as a tool for flexibility while maintaining robustness and readability in Go programs.

5.6. Best Practices for Interface Design

Effective interface design plays a pivotal role in the development of scalable and maintainable software systems. Interfaces serve as the contracts that define interactions between different components, encapsulating behavior while decoupling implementation. Adhering to established best practices ensures that interfaces remain clear, stable, and evolvable over time, ultimately enhancing testability and system robustness.

A fundamental principle in interface design is to express only the essential behavior required by clients, adhering to the Interface Segregation Principle. Interfaces that expose minimal necessary methods enable clients to depend solely on relevant capabilities, reducing unnecessary coupling. This minimizes ripple effects caused by changes and facilitates the creation of focused mocks or stubs during testing. For instance, instead of a monolithic interface with diverse responsibilities, providing several smaller, role-oriented interfaces limits the cognitive load on developers and reduces integration complexity.

When defining method signatures within interfaces, clarity and simplicity are paramount. Method names should be unambiguous and descriptive of the intent without exposing internal implementation details. Parameters should be chosen to convey clear contracts, avoiding excess or optional arguments that introduce ambiguity. Return types must be appropriately specific, avoiding returning overly generic types that shift complexity to the calling code. Utilizing domain-specific value objects rather than primitive types can enhance semantic clarity and enforce validation rules naturally.

API evolution is an intrinsic challenge in long-lived systems. Interfaces must be designed for extensibility without breaking existing clients. One technique is to maintain backward compatibility by adding new interfaces rather than modifying existing ones, allowing implementations to gradually adapt. Default methods in certain modern languages facilitate this by enabling interface evolution without modifying all implementers immediately. Another approach is to version interfaces explicitly, providing clear migration paths. Deprecating methods rather than removing them abruptly preserves stability. Rigorous documentation of interface contracts and version policies further aids client developers in managing changes.

Coupling between components must be minimized to enhance modularity. Interfaces naturally promote loose coupling by abstracting implementations; however, excessive reliance on large interfaces or deep inheritance hierarchies can induce tight coupling. Favor composition over inheritance, encapsulating behavior behind interfaces rather than exposing class hierarchies. Dependency inversion, where high-level modules depend on abstractions rather than concrete classes, strengthens flexibility. Careful control of interface visibility-keeping internal interfaces package- or module-private when feasible-prevents unintended dependencies.

Designing scalable systems benefits from interfaces that both abstract complexity and enable parallel development. Well-defined interfaces act as integration points, allowing teams to work independently on implementations. Interface-driven development, where interfaces are designed before implementation, clarifies requirements and responsibilities early. Employing interface mocks during development and testing accelerates feedback cycles and isolates faults. Moreover, the explicit contracts facilitate system composition, allowing subsystems to evolve independently as long as interface contracts are honored.

Testability is greatly improved by clean interface design. Interfaces decouple the system into interchangeable components, enabling unit testing with minimal reliance on concrete implementations. Dependency injection frameworks leverage interfaces to supply mock or stub components transparently. Interfaces designed with idempotent and side-effect-free methods simplify test scenarios. When interfaces represent asynchronous or event-driven interactions, adopting well-defined callback or future patterns ensures deterministic testing.

Real-world guidelines underscore several specific practices that enhance interface quality:

- Prefer interface-based design early in the development lifecycle, enabling parallel or iterative implementation of components.

- Document interface contracts comprehensively, specifying expected behavior, thread-safety, error conditions, and performance considerations.

- Avoid exposing implementation details, such as internal data structures or mutable state, thus preserving encapsulation.

- Design interfaces to be immutable or stateless when feasible, reducing side effects and simplifying concurrency management.

- Use descriptive naming conventions consistently to indicate interface roles, e.g., `ReadableStream`, `CommandExecutor`, which aids discoverability.

- Avoid method overloads with ambiguous signatures to prevent misuse or confusion.

- Ensure interfaces are cohesive, grouping logically related methods while avoiding unrelated operations that increase coupling.

122

- Place emphasis on stable abstractions, avoiding premature optimization of interface granularity without clear client needs.

Applying these principles does not preclude the necessity for pragmatic trade-offs based on context, such as performance constraints or legacy integration. Nonetheless, consistently maintaining clarity, minimizing coupling, and planning for evolution serve as reliable guides. The synergy between these best practices results in interfaces that underpin scalable, maintainable, and testable software architectures, providing robust foundations for complex system development.

Chapter 6

Concurrency and Parallelism

Embark on a journey through Go's celebrated concurrency model, where lightweight goroutines and channels transform the way you think about scalable, responsive programs. This chapter uncovers how Go harnesses modern hardware, elegantly tackles coordination and synchronization, and arms you with robust patterns for concurrent software that's both safe and fast.

6.1. Goroutines and Scheduling Model

Goroutines are the fundamental unit of concurrency in the Go programming language, designed to enable lightweight, efficient parallelism by abstracting thread management and multiplexing many goroutines onto a smaller set of operating system (OS) threads. Unlike traditional threads, goroutines occupy significantly less memory, allowing thousands to millions of them to coexist and execute concurrently within the same address space. This lightweight nature stems from their minimal initial stack size and runtime-managed growth, combined with a sophisticated scheduler that orchestrates their execution across available processor cores.

When a goroutine is created using the go keyword, the Go runtime spawns a new concurrent function call. This action is not equivalent to creating a distinct OS thread; instead, it registers the function with the internal scheduler that maintains queues of goroutines ready to execute. The goroutine begins with a small stack, typically on the order of a few kilobytes, which expands and shrinks automatically as function calls push or release stack frames. This dynamic stack sizing contrasts with traditional threads, which generally allocate large fixed-size stacks (megabytes in size), thereby conserving memory and enabling the concurrency model to scale.

The Go scheduler follows a cooperative concurrency model customized for the language's runtime environment. The scheduler employs a work-stealing algorithm to distribute goroutines efficiently across multiple OS threads bound to processor cores, referred to as "M" in the Go runtime terminology. These OS threads are dynamically created and destroyed to adapt to workload demands. The scheduler's design includes three primary components: G (goroutine), M (machine or OS thread), and P (processor), where P represents a logical processor context that enables execution. The system maintains a fixed number of P's, corresponding to the maximum parallelism permitted, typically set by the value of GOMAXPROCS.

The interaction between these components follows a clear model:

- **Goroutines (G):** Represent user-level threads encapsulating the function to run, stack state, and associated metadata.

- **Machine (M):** Corresponds directly to an OS thread responsible for executing goroutines.

- **Processor (P):** A logical processor that holds a context and queues for runnable goroutines.

Scheduling proceeds as follows: each P maintains a local run queue of goroutines ready for execution. When an M gets an available P, it continuously dequeues goroutines from P's run queue to execute. If the local queue is empty, the scheduler attempts to steal work from other P queues, balancing load across processors and maintaining high throughput. The use of local queues reduces contention when enqueuing and dequeuing goroutines by confining most operations to a single processor context, thereby improving cache locality and overall system efficiency.

Preemption in the Go scheduler is cooperative and occurs at well-defined safe points, such as function calls or explicit garbage collection checks. This cooperative approach reduces the overhead compared to preemptive thread scheduling, although recent Go versions have introduced improved preemptive capabilities for finer-grained control. When a goroutine blocks (e.g., waiting on I/O or synchronization primitives), the scheduler unwinds its stack to mark it as blocked and retrieves another ready goroutine to execute on the same thread, ensuring that OS threads remain busy. This approach minimizes idle time and maximizes utilization of hardware concurrency.

Goroutines communicate primarily through channels, which provide built-in synchronization primitives enabling safe data exchange and coordination. Channels are integrated deeply into the runtime and scheduler, allowing blocked goroutines to park efficiently and be reawakened when communication is possible. This model abstracts away complex mutexes or condition variables, simplifying parallel programming and reducing the risk of concurrency-related bugs.

One of the key reasons goroutines make parallel programming accessible lies in their transparent concurrency model; programmers create concurrent tasks without managing threads explicitly. The Go runtime automatically handles load balancing, stack management, and scheduling, while goroutines can be started with a single, intuitive keyword:

```
go func() {
    // concurrent task
}()
```

The runtime's lightweight goroutine infrastructure enables massive scalability that traditional threading models cannot achieve efficiently. Moreover, goroutines integrate seamlessly with Go's garbage collector and scheduler, ensuring that system resources are used optimally without programmer intervention.

The scheduler is also responsible for handling asynchronous system calls. Since an OS thread may be blocked on an external call, the runtime utilizes an auxiliary mechanism to maintain responsiveness. If a goroutine is engaged in a blocking system call, the bound M may temporarily detach and allow another M to run on the P, thus preventing the entire scheduler from stalling.

Goroutines form the backbone of Go's concurrency paradigm through their minimal resource footprint, stack management, and efficient scheduling model leveraging the G-M-P architecture. This design suspends explicit thread management complexity from the programmer, allowing a natural and scalable approach to writing highly concurrent applications. The underlying scheduler's combination of work-stealing, cooperative preemption, and dynamic resource management positions Go to achieve both high throughput and low latency in concurrent execution scenarios, making goroutines an exemplary concurrency primitive for modern software development.

6.2. Channels: Buffered and Unbuffered

Channels in Go are core primitives designed to enable safe and structured communication between concurrently executing goroutines. They serve as conduits through which data flows, allowing synchronization and data exchange without explicit locking mechanisms. Channels can be unbuffered or buffered, each exhibiting distinct communication semantics that influence design choices and performance characteristics in concurrent Go programs.

An *unbuffered channel* has no capacity to hold data. A send operation on such a channel blocks until another goroutine is ready to receive from it, ensuring that data is immediately handed off, thus enabling synchronization. Similarly, a receive operation blocks until a value is sent. This rendezvous mechanism enforces direct synchronization between sender and receiver.

The declaration of an unbuffered channel of a specific type, for example integers, uses the syntax

```
ch := make(chan int)
```

Here, the capacity parameter is omitted, indicating an unbuffered channel.

In contrast, a *buffered channel* possesses an internal queue with a fixed capacity. This allows sending goroutines to enqueue values up to the channel's capacity without immediate synchronization with receiving goroutines. Sending blocks only when this buffer is full; receiving blocks only when the buffer is empty.

The syntax to create a buffered channel is

```
ch := make(chan int, 5)
```

which constructs a channel capable of storing up to five integers.

The choice between buffered and unbuffered channels depends on the desired communication pattern and performance considerations. Unbuffered channels are natural for handoff-style synchronization where precise coordination is required. Buffered channels enable asynchronous communication and can improve throughput by decoupling sender and receiver lifetimes, albeit at potential timing trade-offs.

Directional channels enhance type safety by restricting channel operations to either sending or receiving, preventing accidental misuse. For instance, the following function parameter declares a channel that can only be used for sending integers:

```
func send(ch chan<- int, val int) {
    ch <- val
}
```

Conversely, a function accepting a receive-only channel is declared as

```
func receive(ch <-chan int) int {
    return <-ch
}
```

Such directional constraints facilitate clearer communication contracts within the program, promoting safer concurrent patterns and preventing deadlocks arising from unintended operations.

Communication patterns utilizing channels commonly rely on select statements to multiplex multiple concurrent operations. This allows efficient handling of multiple channels, timeouts, or cancellations in a single construct. For example, a select statement waiting on a buffered channel and a timeout channel may appear as follows:

```
select {
case v := <-ch:
    process(v)
case <-time.After(time.Second):
    log.Println("timeout")
}
```

A salient pattern when using buffered channels is the *worker pool*, where a buffered channel acts as a task queue distributing work among a fixed set of goroutines. Buffered channels absorb bursts of incoming requests and smooth scheduling by preventing immediate blocking of requesters.

Consider the following simplified worker pool model:

```
func worker(id int, jobs <-chan int, results chan<- int) {
    for j := range jobs {
        results <- doWork(j)
```

```
        }
}

func main() {
    jobs := make(chan int, 10)
    results := make(chan int, 10)

    for w := 1; w <= 3; w++ {
        go worker(w, jobs, results)
    }

    for j := 1; j <= 5; j++ {
        jobs <- j
    }
    close(jobs)

    for a := 1; a <= 5; a++ {
        <-results
    }
}
```

In this example, the buffered jobs channel allows the main goroutine to enqueue multiple tasks asynchronously, while multiple worker goroutines receive tasks at their own pace.

Conversely, unbuffered channels often serve to implement *pipeline* patterns where each stage of computation is tightly coupled with the next. Because sender and receiver synchronize on each value transfer, this enforces ordered processing and clean handoff semantics suitable for streaming data transformations.

Deadlock considerations are critical in both buffered and unbuffered channels. An unbuffered send without a corresponding concurrent receiver will block indefinitely, and a buffered channel send blocks when the buffer is full. Improper channel closes and misuse of directional constraints can also lead to panic or deadlock. Employing close on a channel signals that no further values will be sent and facilitates graceful termination of range-based receives.

The following example demonstrates safe termination using channel close:

```
func producer(ch chan<- int) {
```

```
    for i := 0; i < 5; i++ {
        ch <- i
    }
    close(ch)
}

func consumer(ch <-chan int) {
    for v := range ch {
        fmt.Println(v)
    }
    fmt.Println("Channel closed, consumer done")
}
```

Once the producer closes the channel, the consumer's range loop exits upon receiving all buffered or in-flight values, enabling clean shutdown.

Go's channels provide powerful abstractions for coordinating goroutines through both unbuffered and buffered variants. Unbuffered channels emphasize direct handoff and synchronization, whereas buffered channels enable asynchronous pipelines and work distribution. Directional types strengthen interface contracts, and idiomatic use of selects and channel close enhance robustness. Mastery of these primitives is instrumental for designing efficient, safe concurrent programs.

6.3. Select Statement and Multiplexing

The `select` statement serves as a fundamental construct for multiplexing communication over multiple channels in concurrent programming environments. By enabling a goroutine to wait on multiple communication operations simultaneously, it permits complex synchronization and coordination patterns that transcend simple sequential channel operations. This section elaborates on the idiomatic use of `select` for managing concurrent workflows, implementing timeouts, and orchestrating communication-driven coordination.

At its core, the `select` statement blocks until one of its case chan-

nels becomes ready for communication (either send or receive).
If multiple cases are ready simultaneously, one is chosen pseudo-
randomly, ensuring fairness and avoiding starvation. A select
statement often includes a default case, allowing non-blocking behavior by immediately executing that case if no other channels are
ready. This built-in multiplexing mechanism forms the foundation
for writing responsive and robust concurrent programs.

Consider two channels, ch1 and ch2, from which a goroutine waits
to receive data:

```
select {
case msg1 := <-ch1:
    // Process msg1 when received on ch1
case msg2 := <-ch2:
    // Process msg2 when received on ch2
}
```

In this pattern, the goroutine blocks until either ch1 or ch2 delivers
a value. This construct is the simplest form of multiplexing, enabling a single thread of control to react dynamically to whichever
channel communicates first.

Timeout management is a critical aspect of resilient concurrent
workflows. The time.After function returns a channel that receives a value after a specified duration, enabling select to implement timeouts gracefully without additional synchronization primitives:

```
select {
case res := <-responseCh:
    // Use res upon successful receipt
case <-time.After(500 * time.Millisecond):
    // Timeout occurred: handle accordingly
}
```

This pattern is idiomatic for preventing indefinite blocking on
channels, providing fail-safe behavior for network requests, I/O
operations, or other interactions with external systems. The
time.After channel triggers after the deadline, allowing the
select to break out with a timeout.

In scenarios where immediate progress is critical and blocking is undesirable, the default clause in select offers a way to poll channels non-blockingly:

```
select {
case msg := <-ch:
    // Process message if ready
default:
    // No message ready; perform alternative action
}
```

The default ensures the select does not block if the channel is empty, allowing the program to continue executing other tasks or retain responsiveness under heavy load conditions.

Complex concurrency requires coordination patterns that involve multiple channels and goroutines. The select statement can be combined with channel closing detection to implement fan-in, fan-out, or cancellation patterns.

For example, a goroutine reading from several input channels until all are closed can elegantly leverage select with checks on channel status:

```
for {
    select {
    case msg, ok := <-ch1:
        if !ok {
            ch1 = nil // Disable case by setting channel to nil
            continue
        }
        // Process msg from ch1
    case msg, ok := <-ch2:
        if !ok {
            ch2 = nil // Disable case for closed channel
            continue
        }
        // Process msg from ch2
    }
    if ch1 == nil && ch2 == nil {
        break // All channels closed, exit loop
    }
}
```

Setting a channel variable to nil disables its case in the select without terminating the loop prematurely. This technique elegantly handles dynamic channel closure during multiplexed operations and ensures orderly shutdown.

In event-driven architectures, `select` enables a single goroutine to act as an event loop waiting on multiple sources—messages, signals, timers—thus reducing context-switch overhead and synchronizing concurrent agents. An example event loop might integrate an external quit signal with multiple data inputs:

```
for {
    select {
    case data := <-dataCh:
        process(data)
    case err := <-errorCh:
        logError(err)
    case <-quitCh:
        return // Graceful shutdown
    }
}
```

This pattern centralizes control flow inside one goroutine and reacts asynchronously to multiple inputs, maintaining a clean separation between communication sources and processing logic.

While powerful, careless use of `select` can lead to subtle bugs:

- *Nil channels must be handled carefully*: a `nil` channel always blocks and disables its `select` case, which can be beneficial for dynamic multiplexing but may cause deadlocks if not properly managed.

- *Avoid busy waiting*: inserting a `default` case without any blocking alternative can result in a busy loop monopolizing CPU cycles.

- *Randomness of case selection*: when multiple cases are ready, the choice is pseudo-random; deterministic ordering using multiple `select` statements or explicit priority channels may be required.

- *Memory leaks due to unconsumed channels*: buffered channels or timers that are never drained can cause resource

leaks; use `Stop` or `Reset` methods and ensure proper drain-
ing strategies for timers.

Understanding these nuances empowers reliable, performant concurrent designs.

Common idiomatic patterns can be summarized as follows:

- Simple multiplexing by waiting on multiple channels without
  a `default` case to enable blocking behavior.

- Implementing timeouts using `time.After` channels to avoid
  indefinite blocking.

- Non-blocking polling with a `default` case to test channel
  readiness.

- Dynamic channel closure handling by setting channels to `nil`
  mid-loop to disable cases.

- Event loops and concurrent coordination via multiple channel cases and quit signaling.

Mastering the `select` statement unlocks highly expressive and efficient concurrent workflows. Its idiomatic usage elegantly balances blocking and responsiveness, enabling concurrency patterns
essential to scalable, high-performance applications.

6.4. Synchronization and State Sharing

Safe sharing of state in concurrent programming is paramount to
ensure correctness and prevent subtle errors such as data races and
deadlocks. Multithreaded programs often require coordinated access to shared resources; this coordination is achieved through synchronization primitives. Among the most fundamental and widely

used tools are mutexes, atomic operations, wait groups, and condition variables. Each serves a specific role in controlling access and signaling between threads.

A *mutex* (short for mutual exclusion) provides exclusive ownership of a critical section of code, preventing concurrent accesses that could corrupt shared data. Typically implemented as a lock, a mutex ensures that only one thread at a time executes the protected critical section. The basic usage pattern involves acquiring the mutex before accessing the shared state and releasing it immediately afterward. This straightforward approach serializes access, preserving invariants within the shared data structure.

```cpp
// Example: Mutex usage in C++
std::mutex mtx;
int shared_counter = 0;

void increment() {
    std::lock_guard<std::mutex> lock(mtx);
    ++shared_counter;  // safe update
}
```

Mutexes are easy to use but must be handled with care to avoid common pitfalls. Deadlocks arise when multiple threads lock several mutexes in inconsistent orders, causing circular wait dependencies. To avoid deadlocks, one best practice is to consistently impose a global order on mutex acquisition and always acquire locks in that order. Additionally, minimizing the scope of locked sections reduces contention and the likelihood of nested locking scenarios.

Atomic operations offer a lower-level synchronization mechanism, providing indivisible operations on shared variables without explicit locking. Modern processors and programming languages provide atomic primitives for common operations such as compare-and-swap, fetch-and-add, and load/store with memory order guarantees. Atomics enable fine-grained synchronization with lower overhead compared to mutexes but require careful design since they do not protect complex invariants on multiple variables.

```
// Example: Using atomic variables in C++
#include <atomic>
std::atomic<int> atomic_counter(0);

void increment_atomic() {
    atomic_counter.fetch_add(1, std::memory_order_relaxed);
}
```

Memory order semantics in atomic operations define constraints on instruction reordering and visibility across threads. Relaxed operations are fastest but provide minimal synchronization, while acquire-release and sequentially consistent orders enforce stronger synchronization guarantees at the cost of performance.

Wait groups and *condition variables* facilitate synchronization based on state changes and inter-thread signaling rather than mutual exclusion of resources. Wait groups (commonly found in languages like Go, or implemented with counters and condition variables in C++) enable one thread to wait for a collection of goroutines or threads to complete, supporting coordinated shutdown or barrier synchronization.

Condition variables allow threads to wait efficiently for a specific condition to become true, avoiding busy-wait loops that waste CPU cycles. Typically paired with a mutex, a thread holding the mutex evaluates a predicate on shared state and, if the predicate is false, waits on the condition variable. Other threads signal the condition variable upon modifying the shared state, triggering a wakeup.

```
// Example: Condition variable in C++
#include <condition_variable>
#include <mutex>

std::mutex mtx;
std::condition_variable cv;
bool ready = false;

void wait_for_ready() {
    std::unique_lock<std::mutex> lock(mtx);
    cv.wait(lock, [] { return ready; });  // wait until ready ==
    true
    // proceed after waking
```

```
}

void signal_ready() {
    {
        std::lock_guard<std::mutex> lock(mtx);
        ready = true;
    }
    cv.notify_one();
}
```

Avoiding *race conditions* requires ensuring that all accesses to shared mutable data are properly synchronized. A race occurs when two or more threads access a variable concurrently, and at least one access is a write without appropriate synchronization. Identifying and eliminating races typically involves adherence to a locking discipline, using atomic operations for simple state changes, and employing tools such as thread sanitizers to detect unsynchronized accesses.

Best practices to prevent race conditions include:

- **Minimize shared state**: Favor designs that reduce or eliminate shared mutable data, such as message-passing concurrency models or immutable data structures.

- **Enforce clear ownership**: Define which thread or component owns certain data, reducing accidental concurrent mutation.

- **Use high-level abstractions**: Prefer well-tested synchronization constructs and thread-safe libraries over ad hoc locking.

- **Document locking protocols**: Clearly specify lock acquisition order and which data each lock protects.

Deadlocks can be mitigated by:

- **Lock order discipline**: Always acquire multiple locks in a consistent global order.

- **Lock timeout and detection**: Employ timed locks with fallback or specialized deadlock detection algorithms.

- **Avoid holding locks during blocking calls**: Prevent self-inflicted contention by releasing locks before invoking potentially blocking operations.

An advanced approach is combining synchronization primitives with higher-level constructs like *futures, promises,* and *thread-safe queues,* which abstract common coordination patterns, reducing direct manipulation of low-level primitives and, consequently, the risk of errors.

In sum, effective synchronization and state sharing in multithreaded programs rest on a comprehensive understanding of primitives like mutexes, atomics, wait groups, and condition variables. Mastery of their semantics, performance trade-offs, and interaction patterns is essential for designing performant and correct concurrent software. Implementers must rigorously apply synchronization disciplines to preempt and resolve race conditions and deadlocks, thereby realizing robust, maintainable multithreaded systems.

6.5. Context and Structured Concurrency

In concurrent programming, managing execution flow, cancellation, timeouts, and data propagation through asynchronous boundaries represents one of the primary challenges. The context package in Go offers a robust abstraction to address this by enabling structural control over concurrent operations. By embedding a Context object within goroutines and other concurrent constructs, developers can coordinate lifetimes, propagate cancellation signals, set deadlines, and convey request-scoped values in a standardized manner.

At its core, a Context is an immutable tree-like structure linked via parent-child relationships. Each Context derives from a parent, inheriting its cancellation signal and deadline constraints. This inheritance facilitates structured concurrency: when a parent context is canceled, all its children are transitively canceled, ensuring that no goroutine prematurely outlives the logical operation it is servicing. The design aligns with the principle that lifecycles of concurrent operations should be deterministically coupled and bounded to prevent resource leaks and orphaned goroutines.

The three principal functionalities of Context can be described as cancellation control, deadline enforcement, and value propagation.

Cancellation

Cancellation in Context is realized through the Done channel. Consumers of a context await the closure of this channel to respond to cancellation events. Cancellation is triggered explicitly via functions such as context.WithCancel, which returns a cancel function; invoking this function signals all derived contexts and goroutines to terminate promptly. Alternatively, cancellation can be implicit, emanating from deadlines or timeouts expiring.

Consider the canonical use of WithCancel:

```
ctx, cancel := context.WithCancel(parentCtx)
defer cancel()

go func(ctx context.Context) {
    select {
    case <-time.After(10 * time.Second):
        // perform work
    case <-ctx.Done():
        // cleanup and return
    }
}(ctx)
```

Here, the spawned goroutine listens concurrently for either work completion or cancellation. Once cancel() is invoked, ctx.Done() closes, signaling the goroutine to abort any further processing. Propagating cancellation coherently avoids the classic pitfall of "dangling" goroutines and tightly bounds resource consumption.

Deadlines and Timeouts

Often, operations must obey temporal constraints to maintain responsiveness or meet service-level objectives. The Context package allows specifying deadlines or relative timeouts using WithDeadline or WithTimeout, respectively. A context with a deadline automatically triggers cancellation once the time is exceeded, simplifying robust timeout handling.

Example of leasing a context with a timeout:

```
ctx, cancel := context.WithTimeout(parentCtx, 5*time.Second)
defer cancel()

select {
case result := <-fetchData(ctx):
    // process result
case <-ctx.Done():
    // handle timeout or cancellation
}
```

By embedding the deadline logic inside the context, spawned goroutines or operations inherently respond to timing constraints without scattering timeout checks throughout the codebase. This approach promotes clean separation of concerns and deterministic resource lifetimes.

Value Propagation Across Goroutines

Context also facilitates the propagation of immutable, request-scoped key-value pairs across API boundaries. Using context.WithValue, callers can associate data such as authentication tokens, credentials, or trace identifiers with a context passed into lower-level functions or goroutines. The responsibility of WithValue is strictly to carry request-scoped information rather than to propagate optional parameters or global states.

For instance:

```
type key int

const userIDKey key = 0

func doWork(ctx context.Context) {
    if uid := ctx.Value(userIDKey); uid != nil {
        fmt.Println("user ID:", uid)
    }
}

ctx := context.WithValue(context.Background(), userIDKey, 42)
doWork(ctx)
```

This pattern enhances modularity by avoiding thread-local or global variables, instead explicitly threading contextual data through call chains.

Interaction With Structured Concurrency

The context package is a fundamental enabler of structured concurrency in Go. By embedding a Context object at the inception of a logical operation and passing it down to all spawned goroutines, the program morphs into an acyclic, tree-structured concurrency graph. The cancellation and timeout features contribute to predictable shutdown of entire concurrency hierarchies, while value propagation ensures consistency and coherence in request-scoped metadata.

Structured concurrency encourages concurrent units of work to be bounded, explicit, and hierarchical. Unlike unstructured concurrency models, where goroutines can be spawned arbitrarily and left uncontrolled, using contexts ties their lifetimes and cancellation logic directly to the originating scope. This approach simplifies debugging, error handling, and resource management by guaranteeing that when a parent operation is abandoned or fails, all associated concurrent work is halted promptly.

Best Practices and Limitations

Proper use of Context demands adhering to certain best practices. Contexts should be passed explicitly as the first argument to func-

CHAPTER 6. CONCURRENCY AND PARALLELISM

tions and methods where cancellation, deadlines, or propagated values matter. They should not be stored in struct fields or globals, preserving immutability and clarity of scope. Furthermore, values stored within contexts must be small, immutable, and request-scoped to prevent misuse and memory leaks.

While Context is instrumental for managing concurrency lifetimes and values, it does not replace other synchronization primitives such as mutexes for shared state protection, nor is it designed for inter-goroutine communication directly—rather, for cancellation and metadata provision. Hence, contexts complement but do not supplant the full suite of concurrency control mechanisms.

In summary, the context package is an essential cornerstone for building well-structured, cancellable, and deadline-aware concurrent programs in Go. By providing a standardized, hierarchical model for control propagation and data sharing, it enables developers to construct safe, predictable concurrent systems that are easier to maintain and reason about.

6.6. Memory Model and Data Races

The Go programming language defines a formal memory model to clarify the semantics of concurrent executions and the conditions under which communication via shared memory is considered safe and well-defined. Understanding this model is essential for developing correct concurrent programs and avoiding subtle, difficult-to-debug errors such as data races.

At its core, the Go memory model establishes a *happens-before* relationship between operations, which dictates the visibility and ordering guarantees of memory accesses in a concurrent environment. A write to a variable has happened-before a read of that variable if the program ensures a synchronization event such as a channel communication, a mutex lock/unlock, or an explicit atomic operation that orders these events. When these synchronization operations link a write and a subsequent read, the read is guaranteed to observe the written value or a later one, providing predictable inter-thread communication.

Formally, the Go memory model specifies that any read of a variable concurrent with a write that is not ordered by happens-before relationships results in undefined behavior known as a *data race*. According to the specification:

> "A data race occurs when two or more goroutines access the same variable concurrently, and at least one of the accesses is a write, and the accesses are not ordered by happens-before."

This definition underscores two critical points. First, any shared memory location accessed without synchronization faces the risk of simultaneous conflicting operations from multiple goroutines. Second, synchronization primitives serve not only to order these operations but also to enforce visibility of changes across goroutines.

Typical synchronization mechanisms in Go include:

- **Channels:** Communications over channels establish happens-before relations by synchronizing the send and receive operations; a send happens-before the corresponding receive.

- **Mutexes:** Lock/unlock pairs on the same mutex order critical section executions, ensuring visibility of shared data updates protected by the mutex.

- **Atomic operations:** Functions from the `sync/atomic` package provide low-level atomic reads, writes, and read-modify-write operations with memory ordering guarantees that establish happens-before edges.

The consequence of violating the memory model through unsynchronized access to shared variables is the emergence of data races. These races induce nondeterministic behavior where values read may be stale or corrupted, resulting in intermittent, hard-to-reproduce failures. The Go runtime includes a `race` detector tool, enabled with the -race compiler flag, that instruments the program to track memory accesses and report conflicting concurrent accesses at runtime.

Practical strategies to avoid data races rely on well-known concurrency design patterns:

Immutable Data. When data is immutable after initialization and exclusively shared with no subsequent writes, data races are inherently impossible. This pattern is preferable for configurations and constants.

Message-Passing Concurrency. Encapsulating shared state inside goroutines communicating only via channels guarantees that at most one goroutine accesses the data at a time. This approach naturally enforces happens-before relations for data reading and modification.

Mutex-Guarded Access. When mutable shared state must be accessed directly, it should be protected by a mutex. Proper locking discipline requires that all accesses, both reads and writes, be bracketed by lock acquisition and release to avoid race conditions.

Atomic Operations. For cases involving individual variables where locking overhead is undesirable, atomic operations provide fine-grained synchronization. They are particularly effective for counters, flags, or pointers shared concurrently.

Understanding happens-before relationships facilitates reasoning about concurrent Go programs. The application of formal reasoning helps prove absence of data races and ensures correct program behavior. For example, if every write to a shared variable happens-before all subsequent reads, then the program is race-free with re-

146

spect to that variable.

The process for reasoning about memory behavior in Go generally involves the following steps:

1. Identify shared variables accessed by multiple goroutines.

2. Determine synchronization events granting ordering guarantees (e.g., channel communications, mutex locks).

3. Establish happens-before relations induced by these events.

4. Verify that all conflicting accesses (read/write or write/write) are ordered by happens-before.

If any pair of conflicting accesses remain unordered, a data race exists and the program must be refactored to enforce proper synchronization.

Notably, the Go memory model prohibits assumptions that sequential consistency or total ordering is guaranteed without explicit synchronization. Writes performed by one goroutine may be observed in differing orders by others absent ordering constraints. Consequently, the source code's apparent order of statements does not imply memory visibility order in concurrent executions, a subtlety critical for correct implementation.

Detecting data races early in the development cycle is feasible via dynamic analysis tools like the Go race detector. However, it is not always comprehensive or efficient for complex systems. Static analysis and formal verification techniques can complement dynamic detection by analyzing all possible execution paths to identify synchronization deficiencies.

Mastering the formal Go memory model and its happens-before construct is foundational to writing safe and reliable concurrent programs. Employing synchronization primitives correctly, following established concurrency patterns, and rigorously analyzing shared state accesses ensure the elimination of data races. This thorough discipline converts the complex semantics of Go concurrency into predictable and maintainable parallel implementations.

6.7. Concurrency Patterns and Idioms

Go's concurrency model is centered on goroutines and channels, enabling developers to express sophisticated concurrent workflows succinctly and efficiently. Beyond basic goroutine launches and channel communications, proven concurrency patterns embody best practices that help harness the power of Go's primitives while maintaining readability, scalability, and robustness. This section synthesizes several canonical patterns— worker pools, pipelines, fan-in/fan-out—and introduces crucial idioms for error handling and cancellation, delineating how these integrate to form resilient concurrent applications.

Worker Pools

Worker pools implement controlled parallelism by distributing workloads across a fixed number of worker goroutines. This pattern is essential when the cost of spawning excessive goroutines outweighs benefits or when access to limited resources must be throttled. A pool typically operates with two channels: a job input channel to receive tasks and a results channel to collect outputs.

Consider a scenario processing computationally intensive tasks received from an external source. The worker pool structure ensures bounded concurrency and orderly result aggregation:

```
type Job struct {
    ID      int
    Payload interface{}
}

type Result struct {
    JobID int
    Data  interface{}
```

```
}

func worker(jobs <-chan Job, results chan<- Result, wg *sync.
    WaitGroup) {
    defer wg.Done()
    for job := range jobs {
        // Perform computation or I/O-bound processing
        result := process(job)
        results <- Result{JobID: job.ID, Data: result}
    }
}

func main() {
    jobs := make(chan Job)
    results := make(chan Result)
    var wg sync.WaitGroup

    const numWorkers = 5
    for i := 0; i < numWorkers; i++ {
        wg.Add(1)
        go worker(jobs, results, &wg)
    }

    go func() {
        for i := 0; i < 100; i++ {
            jobs <- Job{ID: i}
        }
        close(jobs)
    }()

    go func() {
        wg.Wait()
        close(results)
    }()

    for result := range results {
        fmt.Printf("Processed job %d: %v\n", result.JobID, result
    .Data)
    }
}
```

This approach balances throughput and resource utilization. The closing of channels signals completion, ensuring no goroutines remain blocked indefinitely.

Pipelines

Pipelines compose streams of stages, each performing a distinct transformation or processing step on the data. Each stage runs concurrently as a goroutine and communicates exclusively through channels, allowing the decomposition of complex flows into well-defined, composable units.

A simple pipeline with three stages: generation, transformation, and output, demonstrates this idiom:

```
func gen(nums ...int) <-chan int {
    out := make(chan int)
    go func() {
        defer close(out)
        for _, n := range nums {
            out <- n
        }
    }()
    return out
}

func sq(in <-chan int) <-chan int {
    out := make(chan int)
    go func() {
        defer close(out)
        for n := range in {
            out <- n * n
        }
    }()
    return out
}

func main() {
    nums := gen(2, 3, 4)
    sqs := sq(nums)
    for n := range sqs {
        fmt.Println(n)
    }
}
```

The core advantages include inherent parallelism, modularity, and clear data-flow semantics. Channels serve as well-defined hand-offs, reducing shared state and synchronization complexity.

Fan-In and Fan-Out Patterns

Fan-out distributes workload among multiple concurrent workers; fan-in consolidates results from multiple sources into a single channel. These patterns frequently combine to implement scalable concurrent processing pipelines.

Fan-out example: splitting input to multiple workers competing for jobs.

Fan-in example: merging multiple output channels into a single channel for unified processing.

A typical fan-in implementation leverages goroutines to multiplex multiple input channels:

```go
func fanIn(channels ...<-chan int) <-chan int {
    var wg sync.WaitGroup
    out := make(chan int)

    output := func(c <-chan int) {
        defer wg.Done()
        for n := range c {
            out <- n
        }
    }

    wg.Add(len(channels))
    for _, c := range channels {
        go output(c)
    }

    go func() {
        wg.Wait()
        close(out)
    }()
    return out
}
```

This composability is crucial for building flexible concurrency topologies. Fan-in/fan-out patterns exploit Go's channel semantics to streamline load balancing and result aggregation without explicit locks.

Robust Error Handling and Cancellation

Distributed concurrent operations intensify the complexity of error handling and cancellation propagation. Go's context package provides a standard mechanism to propagate deadlines, cancellations, and errors across goroutine hierarchies coherently.

Embedding a context.Context in worker pools, pipelines, or fan-out goroutines allows graceful shutdown triggered by upstream errors or timeouts:

```
func worker(ctx context.Context, jobs <-chan Job, results chan<-
    Result, errors chan<- error) {
    for {
        select {
        case <-ctx.Done():
            return
        case job, ok := <-jobs:
            if !ok {
                return // no more jobs
            }
            result, err := processWithError(job)
            if err != nil {
                select {
                case errors <- err:
                case <-ctx.Done():
                }
                return
            }
            select {
            case results <- result:
            case <-ctx.Done():
                return
            }
        }
    }
}
```

The parent orchestrator listens on the error channel and cancels the context upon detection, cascading cancellation to all workers:

```
func run(ctx context.Context, jobs []Job) error {
    ctx, cancel := context.WithCancel(ctx)
    defer cancel()

    jobChan := make(chan Job)
    resultChan := make(chan Result)
    errChan := make(chan error, 1)

    var wg sync.WaitGroup
    for i := 0; i < numWorkers; i++ {
        wg.Add(1)
        go func() {
            defer wg.Done()
            worker(ctx, jobChan, resultChan, errChan)
        }()
    }

    go func() {
```

```
        for _, job := range jobs {
            select {
            case jobChan <- job:
            case <-ctx.Done():
                break
            }
        }
        close(jobChan)
    }()

    go func() {
        wg.Wait()
        close(resultChan)
    }()

    select {
    case err := <-errChan:
        cancel()
        return err
    case <-ctx.Done():
        return ctx.Err()
    }
}
```

This idiom ensures deterministic resource cleanup and error handling propagation, mitigating common pitfalls of concurrent programming such as goroutine leaks and silent failures.

- Worker pools regulate resource utilization while leveraging parallel hardware.

- Pipelines decompose complex data transformations into manageable concurrent stages.

- Fan-in/fan-out flexibly redistributes workloads and aggregates results.

- Context-based cancellation and error propagation address reliability concerns inherent in concurrent execution.

Mastering these idioms unlocks Go's expressive concurrency abilities, enabling concise, maintainable, and performant systems. Practical applications-from network servers to data processing frameworks-arise naturally by combining these building blocks within idiomatic, channel-driven designs.

Chapter 7

Error Handling and Robustness

*Peer behind the scenes of Go's pragmatic approach to failure—
and learn why its culture of explicit error management leads directly to resilient, production-ready software. This chapter reveals not just the how, but the why of Go's error strategies, equip-
ping you with the tools and judgement to build systems that recover gracefully and communicate problems clearly.*

7.1.   Errors as Values

Go's approach to error handling diverges fundamentally from traditional exception-based models common in many contemporary
programming languages. Instead of treating errors as exceptional
control flows that disrupt normal execution, Go treats errors as ordinary values. This design philosophy promotes explicitness, simplicity, and composability in error management, enabling developers to handle failures as part of the program's normal data flow.

At the core of this philosophy is the `error` interface, a minimal interface type defined in the standard library:

```
type error interface {
    Error() string
}
```

This interface represents an error as any type that implements the `Error()` method, returning a descriptive message. Unlike exceptions or checked errors, the `error` type imposes no special runtime semantics; instead, it relies on the discipline of returning and inspecting error values explicitly. This allows errors to be propagated as pieces of data, passed around, wrapped, or inspected just like any other values.

The motivation behind treating errors as values is multifaceted:

- **Simplicity and clarity.** By making error handling explicit in function signatures-typically returning an `error` as the last return value-callers are compelled to consider and address failure conditions directly. This explicitness reduces hidden control flow and increases the readability of interaction patterns.

- **Composability and flexibility.** Since errors are normal values, they can be richly composed and manipulated. Developers can wrap errors to add context, create sentinel errors for comparison, or define custom types that implement `error` to embed additional semantics.

- **Improved testability and debugging.** Test functions can assert on specific error values or error messages, facilitating precise unit tests. The absence of implicit control flows means that each error path is plainly visible, enhancing reasoning about failure modes.

- **Avoiding hidden control paths.** Unlike exceptions, which may cause control to jump unpredictably, Go's explicit error returns anchor all error handling within linear control flow, simplifying static and dynamic analysis.

Consider a typical Go function signature incorporating error handling:

```
func ReadConfig(filename string) (*Config, error) {
    file, err := os.Open(filename)
    if err != nil {
        return nil, err
    }
    defer file.Close()

    config, err := ParseConfig(file)
    if err != nil {
        return nil, err
    }
    return config, nil
}
```

This example illustrates how error values flow naturally as ordinary function results. Upon encountering an error, the function returns it immediately, allowing callers to react explicitly. No language-level construct automatically propagates or catches errors; this is left to the programmer's control.

One compelling feature resulting from this approach is the use of sentinel errors and error wrapping. Sentinel errors are predefined error values or variables that represent particular failure conditions, enabling direct comparison at call sites:

```
var ErrNotFound = errors.New("not found")

func Lookup(key string) (string, error) {
    if !exists(key) {
        return "", ErrNotFound
    }
    return getValue(key), nil
}
```

Callers can then check for specific errors explicitly:

```
val, err := Lookup("foo")
if err == ErrNotFound {
    // Handle missing key scenario
}
```

In addition, the `fmt.Errorf` function introduced the concept of wrapping errors with additional context using the `%w` verb, which enhances error introspection and debugging:

```
if err != nil {
    return fmt.Errorf("failed to read config %s: %w", filename,
        err)
}
```

This pattern preserves the original error while annotating contextual information, facilitating error unwrapping and classification through the `errors.Is` and `errors.As` functions introduced in Go 1.13.

The implications of modeling errors as values extend deeply into testing. Tests can use precise assertions on error values to verify both the occurrence and nature of failures, supporting fine-grained control:

```
func TestLookup_NotFound(t *testing.T) {
    _, err := Lookup("missing")
    if err != ErrNotFound {
        t.Fatalf("expected ErrNotFound, got %v", err)
    }
}
```

This clarity reduces reliance on brittle checks such as inspecting strings, thereby strengthening correctness guarantees and maintainability.

Furthermore, this style composes naturally with Go's `defer`, `panic`, and `recover` constructs. Panics are reserved for truly exceptional, unrecoverable conditions-algorithmic invariants or programmer errors-while routine failure modes are captured by explicit error values. This separation of concerns clarifies the expected control-flow properties and encourages robust, predictable error handling strategies.

Overall, Go's errors-as-values philosophy produces codebases with transparent and straightforward error flows, enabling effective reasoning, modularity, and testing. By integrating error information directly into the call-return paradigm, this approach encourages developers to confront failures explicitly rather than as side effects or exceptional cases, improving program reliability and clarity without sacrificing performance or expressiveness.

7.2. Custom Error Types and Wrapping

In advanced Go programming, error handling extends beyond the typical use of predefined error values. Creating custom error types enables precise control over the error structure, embedding additional context, and facilitating domain-specific error distinctions. Custom errors become pivotal when an application requires tailored behavior or when errors serve as signals within complex control flows.

A custom error type in Go is traditionally implemented as a struct satisfying the error interface by implementing the Error() string method. Additionally, including extra fields allows embedding contextual information, such as error codes, operation names, or input parameters, which can greatly assist in diagnosis and remediation. Consider the following canonical example:

```
type PathError struct {
    Op   string // operation, e.g. "open"
    Path string // file or resource path
    Err  error  // underlying error
}

func (e *PathError) Error() string {
    return fmt.Sprintf("%s %s: %v", e.Op, e.Path, e.Err)
}
```

This struct conveys not only the high-level nature of the failure (e.g., file opening) but also references the underlying error that caused the failure (Err). This composition facilitates granular inspection of error causes and supports rich error messages that are informative and actionable.

Beyond mere augmentation, Go 1.13 introduced standardized error

159

wrapping, which implicitly improves error propagation patterns by retaining causal chains of failures. Wrapping an error preserves the original error while adding context as the stack unwinds, providing layered insight into what failed and why. The fmt.Errorf function, embellished with the %w verb, efficiently accomplishes this:

```
if err != nil {
    return fmt.Errorf("read config: %w", err)
}
```

This wrapping mechanism creates an error chain where each layer represents additional context triggered by successive function calls. To work effectively with wrapped errors, errors.Is and errors.As were introduced to facilitate inspection within these chains.

The function errors.Is enables identifying whether a specific error occurs anywhere within the wrapping chain, abstracting away the complexity of nested wrapping. For example, if a caller wants to check whether an error corresponds to io.EOF despite multiple wraps, errors.Is returns true if io.EOF appears at any wrapped layer:

```
if errors.Is(err, io.EOF) {
    // Handle EOF specifically
}
```

Similarly, errors.As performs a type assertion through the wrapping hierarchy. It is invaluable for extracting specific custom error types, especially when additional fields carry meaningful details. For instance:

```
var pathErr *PathError
if errors.As(err, &pathErr) {
    fmt.Printf("failed operation: %s on %s\n", pathErr.Op,
        pathErr.Path)
}
```

This idiom enables developers to conditionally branch error-handling logic based on precise error typologies, leveraging polymorphism and encapsulated data without fragile string parsing or error code matching.

Constructing composable and inspectable error hierarchies relies on consistently wrapping errors and defining custom types that expose meaningful exported properties. When designing such error types, it is crucial to embed the original error (by field or via fmt.Errorf wrapping) to preserve error chains, enabling robust downstream inspection.

Moreover, in some scenarios, layering helper methods on custom errors can provide even richer introspection. For example, implementing an Unwrap() error method on a custom error type signals to Go's wrapping mechanism and tooling how to traverse the chain:

```
func (e *PathError) Unwrap() error {
    return e.Err
}
```

Defining Unwrap() complements the use of fmt.Errorf and is especially important when custom errors embed multiple nested errors or manage more complex causality graphs.

A practical illustration of error wrapping together with custom types is evident in network or file operations, where errors may arise from multiple subsystems. Wrapping errors at each level with meaningful context preserves the diagnostic trail and can drastically reduce time spent debugging. The idiomatic pattern encourages immediate wrapping near the source:

```
func ReadFile(name string) error {
    f, err := os.Open(name)
    if err != nil {
        return &PathError{"open", name, err}
    }
    defer f.Close()

    // proceed reading...
}
```

By returning a PathError embedded with the lower-level os.Open error, the caller gains clear insight into both the operation and file involved, which can then be further wrapped upstream.

Custom error types paired with the wrapping features and introspection APIs of the Go standard library form an essential foundation for scalable, maintainable, and debuggable Go applications. They empower developers to build layered, composable error-handling strategies while maintaining the ability to detect and analyze root failure causes with precision.

7.3. Error Propagation and Contextualization

In complex software systems, error propagation and contextualization play a pivotal role in maintaining robustness and facilitating effective debugging. When errors occur, especially within multi-layered programs, it is insufficient to merely signal failure; the error reporting must carry comprehensive contextual information, allowing developers to trace the origin and understand the sequence of failure.

Error propagation refers to the systematic forwarding of error information through the layers of a program. Rather than reverting to generic exceptions or boolean flags, advanced error propagation methods preserve error metadata, including source location, operation parameters, and state at the time of error. Contextualization enriches these error reports with domain-specific insights, such as transaction identifiers, user session data, or functional annotations, which are indispensable for root-cause analysis.

Structured Error Types and Wrapping

A foundational technique involves designing structured error types which encapsulate both the cause and the context of failure. Such error types often implement interfaces supporting the retrieval of original errors and additional metadata. A common pattern is error wrapping, where successive layers add contextual information by embedding one error within another.

For example, consider a scenario in a multi-layered network application: a low-level socket connection fails, triggering a higher-level protocol error, which subsequently causes a service-layer transaction failure. Each layer wraps the error, appending context before repropagating it:

```
type AppError struct {
    Msg      string
    Cause    error
    Context  map[string]interface{}
}

func (e *AppError) Error() string {
    return fmt.Sprintf("%s: %v", e.Msg, e.Cause)
}

// Propagating with added context
func dbQuery() error {
    if err := lowLevelNetworkCall(); err != nil {
        return &AppError{
            Msg:   "DB Query failed",
            Cause: err,
            Context: map[string]interface{}{
                "query": "SELECT * FROM users WHERE id=42",
            },
        }
    }
    return nil
}
```

This recursive encapsulation allows a stack of error contexts that can be inspected to reveal the entire path through the system where the problem occurred.

Error Annotation via Contextual Metadata

Augmenting errors with contextual metadata goes beyond textual messages. Contextual key-value pairs can represent variable states, configuration parameters, or environmental conditions at the time of failure. Modern languages and frameworks often provide mechanisms to associate such structured data with errors.

This annotation transforms errors from mere textual descriptions into rich diagnostic objects that can be filtered, searched, and analyzed systematically. For instance, logging frameworks supporting structured data allow correlating errors with affected users, performance metrics, or temporal patterns, vastly improving incident triage and resolution.

Propagating Errors with Context in Functional Paradigms

Functional programming paradigms advocate explicit error handling via types like `Either`, `Option`, or monadic constructs, which formalize error propagation without resorting to exceptions. In functional chains, errors are propagated while preserving the computational context.

A typical technique involves attaching contextual information as part of the monadic value that flows through a computation pipeline. This ensures that when an error occurs, all accumulated context prior to failure is readily accessible. For example, in Haskell-like pseudocode:

```
type Context = Map String String

data Result a = Success a Context | Failure String Context

bind :: Result a -> (a -> Result b) -> Result b
bind (Failure msg ctx) _ = Failure msg ctx
bind (Success val ctx) f =
    case f val of
        Success val' ctx'   -> Success val' (merge ctx ctx')
        Failure msg ctx'    -> Failure msg (merge ctx ctx')
```

This approach inherently supports error contextualization, where every function contributes to the cumulative context until a failure is reached.

Stack Traces and Source Attribution

Automatic capture and propagation of stack traces remain invaluable tools for error contextualization. They provide structural insight into the sequence of function invocations leading to failure.

Some modern runtimes and libraries support lazy stack trace evaluation or selective capture to minimize overhead while preserving diagnostic power.

Augmenting these traces with source code position, including filename, line number, and function name, further enhances actionable information. Techniques such as embedding call-site context at the moment an error is wrapped or annotating the error with execution state snapshots improve diagnostic precision.

Recovery Strategies Informed by Context

Accurate contextualization of errors facilitates more nuanced recovery strategies. Instead of generic retry or abort behavior, the program can discriminate among error types and their circumstances. For instance, transient network failures with certain error codes might trigger scheduled retries, whereas logic errors in business rules may lead to immediate abort and alerting.

In multithreaded or distributed systems, context propagation also allows for tracing correlated errors across components. Propagation of contextual identifiers, such as correlation IDs or trace spans, enables distributed tracing frameworks to reconstruct the error journey through microservices or parallel tasks.

Design Patterns for Effective Error Propagation

Several design principles enhance error propagation efficacy:

- **Fail Early with Rich Context:** Capture and annotate error context as close as possible to the failure origin before passing control upward.

- **Immutable Error Objects:** Use immutable error representations to prevent accidental loss or mutation of context.

- **Separation of Concerns:** Distinguish between error signaling and logging; propagation focuses on programmatic handling, whereas logging formats and delivers information to operators.

- **Composability:** Design error types and context attachment to compose naturally, allowing layers to merge contexts without loss.

Practical Illustration: Annotating and Propagating Errors in a Multilayer API

Consider a REST API server handling client requests, with several internal layers: authentication, validation, business logic, and data persistence. An authentication failure should propagate with user identity information and token state. Validation errors should include input parameters and schema details. Business logic errors carry transaction IDs and relevant temporal data.

At each layer, errors are wrapped with specific context before propagation:

```
class ApiError(Exception):
    def __init__(self, message, *, cause=None, context=None):
        super().__init__(message)
        self.cause = cause
        self.context = context or {}

def authenticate(token):
    if not token.is_valid():
        raise ApiError("Authentication failed", context={"
    token_id": token.id})

def validate_request(data):
    if not schema.validate(data):
        raise ApiError("Validation failed", context={"fields":
    schema.errors})

def process_request(data, token):
    try:
        authenticate(token)
        validate_request(data)
        # business logic...
    except ApiError as e:
        # Attach broader request context and re-raise
        raise ApiError("Request processing error", cause=e,
                    context={"request_id": data.get("id")})
```

The resulting error object, when handled at an outermost layer,

166

contains a chain of causes along with layered contextual information. Inspection tools or log processors can then extract these nested contexts to produce an articulate failure narrative.

Robust error propagation and contextualization mechanisms form the bedrock of resilient and maintainable software. By systematically carrying rich, structured information from the failure point through the program's layers, developers gain precise insight into error origins and system state. Such insights drastically reduce debugging time and improve operational incident response, enabling systems to achieve higher reliability and clarity in failure modes.

7.4. Recoverable vs. Unrecoverable Errors

In robust system design, a central challenge lies in distinguishing between recoverable errors—unexpected but manageable deviations from normal operation—and unrecoverable errors, conditions severe enough to warrant immediate cessation of processing. This distinction is crucial for building software that gracefully navigates failures without sacrificing reliability or maintainability.

Recoverable errors represent situations in which the system can detect a failure condition, attempt corrective measures, or notify the caller of the problem, enabling the overall system to continue functioning. Examples include failed file reads due to transient I/O issues, invalid user input, or network timeouts. Proper handling of such errors prevents silent data corruption and allows for meaningful recovery strategies such as retries, fallbacks, or user intervention.

In contrast, unrecoverable errors correspond to conditions that violate fundamental assumptions of the program or represent irreparable inconsistencies in internal state. These are often systemic faults indicating bugs, resource exhaustion, or logical contradictions. Typical examples include null pointer dereferences, out-of-bounds array access, or invariants broken by concurrent data races. Attempting recovery in these scenarios risks propagating corruption, leading to unpredictable behavior and exacerbated failures.

A common idiom for signaling unrecoverable errors in several modern programming languages is the *panic-recover* mechanism. This approach deliberately aborts the normal control flow at the point of fault using a panic (or throw), unwinding the stack until a designated recovery handler intercepts the panic and attempts remediation or cleanup before resuming safe execution paths. This idiom imposes a clear demarcation between ordinary error handling—expressed via explicit return values or error types—and exceptional control transfers for unrecoverable conditions.

Consider the following idiomatic pattern in a hypothetical language supporting panic and recover constructs:

```
function readConfig(file):
    if not file.exists():
        panic("Configuration file missing")
    config = parse(file)
    if config.invalid():
        panic("Malformed configuration")
    return config

function main():
    try:
        config = readConfig("app.cfg")
        startService(config)
    except Panic as e:
        log("Fatal startup error: " + e.message)
        exit(1)
```

Here, the functions assert critical assumptions—presence and validity of configuration—using panic for unrecoverable errors. The main function's recovery block (except Panic) catches the panic, logs, and terminates the process, preserving system integrity and signaling failure explicitly.

In contrast, recoverable errors should be handled locally and propagated using explicit error values or result types enabling the caller to decide on remediation strategies. For example:

```
function readData(source) -> Result<Data, Error>:
    data = source.fetch()
    if data == null:
        return Error("Data not available")
    if !data.valid():
        return Error("Invalid data")
    return Ok(data)

function process():
    result = readData(remoteSource)
    if result.isError():
        log("Warning: " + result.error())
        useFallback()
    else:
        processData(result.value())
```

This pattern avoids panics for routine failures and empowers the caller to handle errors appropriately, balancing reliability and responsiveness.

A critical consideration in error design is avoiding silent failures, which occur when errors go unnoticed or unreported, leading to cascading problems. Ensuring errors are communicated visibly—via logs, explicit returns, or asserted conditions—is essential. Equally important is avoiding unduly catastrophic exits on recoverable errors, which impair user experience and system availability.

Robust system design thus emerges from a precise classification of error domains. The design process entails:

- **Defining invariants:** Identify core assumptions and conditions that must never be violated at runtime. Breaches trigger unrecoverable errors.

- **Enumerating error types:** Distinguish recoverable failures from exceptional faults at the type and interface level.

- **Employing appropriate signaling:** Use return codes, result types, or error objects for recoverable errors, while reserving panic or exceptions for invariant violations.

- **Composing recovery layers:** Multiple tiers of error handling, from localized retries and fallbacks to a top-level panic handler, enforce resilience.

- **Instrumenting visibility:** Log error occurrences systematically, ensuring failures are detectable and diagnosable without flooding output.

An example strategy is encapsulating recoverable errors within a Result or Either monadic type, which forces the caller to handle or propagate errors explicitly. Unrecoverable errors, by contrast, bypass ordinary returns, utilizing language-level panic or exception mechanisms to escalate immediately.

Signal-based and resource-failure errors often fall in a gray area and require contextual judgment. A network failure during a noncritical data fetch may warrant recoverable handling (e.g., retries), whereas memory exhaustion during query execution represents an unrecoverable situation that necessitates panic.

In concurrent and distributed systems, designing error handling to avoid silent failures becomes especially challenging. Failures must be detected within timing bounds and propagated explicitly across boundaries. Combining comprehensive error types, panic-recover idioms, and strategic restarts contributes to robust fault tolerance.

The principle focus when designing error management is to codify clear boundaries between:

1. *Errors to be handled*: expected consequences of uncertain environments or user input, requiring documented recovery protocols.

2. *Truly exceptional situations*: fundamental correctness violations demanding immediate program termination or controlled restart.

Adhering strictly to this division provides predictability, improves software quality, and enables systematic reasoning about error propagation and recovery. The panic-recover idiom, employed prudently alongside expressive error return types, equips developers with a flexible toolkit for realizing these goals, avoiding both silent degradations and disproportionately catastrophic failures.

7.5. Best Practices in Error Handling

Error handling represents a critical dimension of software robustness, maintainability, and usability. Well-crafted error management goes beyond mere detection and recovery; it is a core design consideration that influences the clarity of the codebase, developer experience, and system diagnostics.

A fundamental principle in error handling is to treat errors as first-class entities, not afterthoughts or incidental outcomes. This mindset translates into specific practices for coding, documenting, and logging error paths that collectively enhance system comprehension and reliability.

Explicit Error-Returning Interfaces

One pervasive best practice is to design APIs with explicit error returns rather than implicit exception throwing or silent failure modes. This approach bestows transparency by making error conditions visible and integral to function contracts.

In languages supporting multiple return values, such as Go, a typical pattern is:

```
func ReadConfig(path string) (Config, error) {
    config, err := readFromFile(path)
    if err != nil {
        return Config{}, err
    }
    return config, nil
}
```

This explicit paradigm encourages callers to handle errors immediately or propagate them consciously, avoiding overlooked failures. For languages relying on exceptions, clear documentation and judicious use of checked exceptions (where available) can similarly enforce handling discipline.

Clarity Through Minimal and Focused Error Propagation

Error propagation should be concise and targeted. Avoid cluttering the codebase with error handling that obscures the main logic flow. One effective pattern is to centralize error handling decisions within narrowly scoped blocks, deferring detailed processing until higher levels where context is richer.

For example, in C++ a common idiom involves catching exceptions close to application boundaries for meaningful recovery or user notification, while allowing library internals to throw with minimal interference. This reduces duplicated error checks and improves readability.

Error Types and Enriched Context

Utilizing strong, descriptive error types enhances clarity and debuggability. Employ custom error classes or structs that encapsulate not only the error cause but also relevant context. Contextual information may include operation details, parameter values, and error provenance (e.g., system call, network, or domain-specific failure).

A salient example in Rust uses the `thiserror` crate to define rich, typed errors:

```
#[derive(Debug, thiserror::Error)]
pub enum ConfigError {
    #[error("file not found: {path}")]
    FileNotFound { path: String },

    #[error("parse failure at line {line}")]
    ParseError { line: usize },
}
```

Such types enable precise pattern matching and tailored responses,

172

minimizing ambiguity.

Comprehensive and Concise Documentation of Error Contracts

Explicitly documenting error pathways and guarantees is critical. API documentation should specify:

- The conditions under which errors occur.

- The type and semantics of returned errors.

- Whether errors signal recoverable or fatal conditions.

- Recommendations for handling or propagation.

This clarity ensures client developers understand how to safely and effectively respond to failure, preventing misuse and improving integration quality. Inline comments enrich code readability but should complement rather than replace formal API documentation.

Idiomatic and Contextual Logging Practices

Robust logging is indispensable during error conditions, enabling retrospective diagnosis and real-time alerting. Best practices in logging error paths include:

- Logging at the appropriate granularity: capture sufficient context without overwhelming logs.

- Using structured logs with key-value pairs for consistent parsing and filtering by observability systems.

- Avoiding logging sensitive or personally identifiable information.

- Correlating logs with trace or request identifiers to reconstruct behavior across distributed components.

- Employing different log levels (e.g., ERROR, WARN, INFO) carefully; log errors at the ERROR level while leaving recoverable incidents at WARN or INFO.

An example in Python using the structlog library demonstrates structured error logging:

```
import structlog

log = structlog.get_logger()

try:
    config = load_config("config.yaml")
except FileNotFoundError as e:
    log.error("configuration load failed", error=str(e), path="
    config.yaml")
    raise
```

Structured logs at error points augment operational observability, accelerating resolution times.

Balancing Failure Transparency and API Simplicity

While explicit error handling elevates robustness, excessively verbose error propagation can degrade API ergonomics. Striking a balance requires designing error types and handlers that convey necessary detail while remaining simple to use. This balance can be achieved by:

- Grouping related errors under umbrella types or hierarchies.

- Providing wrapper functions to abstract common error checks and transformations.

- Allowing optional retrieval of extended error details, preserving clean default control flows.

Avoiding Anti-Patterns and Maintaining Consistency

Common anti-patterns that undermine error handling quality include:

174

- Ignoring return errors or swallowing exceptions silently.

- Overusing error codes or magic values without clear semantics.

- Mixing error handling strategies inconsistently across modules.

- Excessive nesting of error handling blocks and callbacks that reduce readability.

Establishing and enforcing consistent project-wide error handling policies helps attenuate these issues.

Summary of Effective Error Handling Patterns

- Design APIs that incorporate errors as explicit return types or well-documented exceptions.

- Propagate errors minimally and contextually, centralizing handling logic where feasible.

- Use rich, typed error definitions that carry contextual metadata.

- Document error contracts comprehensively to guide consumers.

- Implement structured, contextual logging that integrates with observability tools.

- Balance transparency with simplicity to maintain clear yet robust interfaces.

- Avoid silence, inconsistency, and clutter in error management pathways.

Together, these best practices cultivate a culture of deliberate, transparent, and maintainable error handling that substantially enhances software quality across its lifecycle.

7.6. Testing Error Conditions

Robust software development mandates not only implementing comprehensive error handling but also thoroughly testing these error paths to verify correctness and resilience. Error conditions tend to be less frequently exercised in typical execution, yet failures in these paths can lead to critical system breakdowns. Strategies for testing error conditions encompass systematic assertions, simulation of fault scenarios, and verification that recovery mechanisms perform as intended. Emphasizing rigorous testing of error paths ensures that assumptions within error handling logic hold true and that unexpected states do not propagate unnoticed.

Assertions serve as internal self-checks embedded in code to validate invariants and assumptions, especially after error detection and handling operations. As error handling often involves state mutation or resource management, assertions can confirm that the system remains in a consistent and expected condition. For example, after closing a file descriptor upon detecting a read error, an assertion can verify that the descriptor is marked invalid or released properly.

```
FILE *fp = fopen("data.txt", "r");
if (fp == NULL) {
    perror("File open failed");
    // No valid file pointer; further reads forbidden
    assert(fp == NULL);
    return -1;
}

// Proceed with reading file
int result = fread(buffer, sizeof(char), size, fp);
if (result < size) {
    fprintf(stderr, "Partial read: %d bytes\n", result);
    fclose(fp);
    // Confirm that file pointer is closed
    assert(fp != NULL);  // This will now fail if not closed
     properly
}
```

Assertions in this context act as guards during development and testing phases. In production, assertions may be disabled, so critical error handling verification should not rely solely on them but also be included in explicit test procedures.

Real-world error occurrences such as memory allocation failures, I/O errors, or network timeouts are nondeterministic and challenging to reproduce consistently. Testing these conditions requires artificial simulation to force error paths. Common approaches include:

- **Dependency Injection of Fault Generators**: Replacing real dependencies with mocks or stubs that simulate failures. For instance, substituting the memory allocator with a controlled version that returns NULL for specific allocation requests enables testing out-of-memory handling.

- **Fault Injection Frameworks**: Specialized frameworks allow targeted injection of faults at runtime, such as forcing file system errors or network packet drops. These tools facilitate systematic exploration of error behavior without modifying production code directly.

- **Error Return Value Manipulation**: Temporarily patching functions or overriding system calls to provoke specific error return codes, e.g., injecting EIO during disk operations or simulating ENOMEM during memory requests.

Consider unit testing a function that allocates memory, then reads a configuration file:

```
typedef void* (*malloc_func_t)(size_t);
malloc_func_t test_malloc = malloc;

void *test_wrapper_malloc(size_t size) {
    if (simulate_alloc_failure) {
        return NULL; // Simulate allocation failure
    }
    return malloc(size);
}

int read_config(const char *path) {
    void *buffer = test_malloc(BUFFER_SIZE);
```

```
    if (!buffer) {
        fprintf(stderr, "Memory allocation failed\n");
        return -1;
    }
    // Proceed with file read...
    free(buffer);
    return 0;
}
```

By toggling `simulate_alloc_failure` during tests, the error path becomes reproducible, enabling validation of recovery code and messaging.

Verification extends beyond triggering errors; it requires thorough observation of outcomes to ensure the system adheres to the intended fault tolerance policy. Reliable error handling means:

- **Correct Error Propagation**: Ensuring errors are neither swallowed silently nor converted into misleading states. Testing must confirm that functions return appropriate error codes or throw correct exceptions.

- **Resource Integrity**: Error handling should not cause resource leaks, such as open file descriptors, memory leaks, or dangling locks. Tools like valgrind, sanitizers, or dedicated resource tracking enable automatic detection.

- **State Consistency Post-Error**: System state variables and invariants must remain coherent. For example, after a failed database operation, transactions must be either rolled back or left in a valid committed state.

- **Practicing Negative Testing**: Negative test cases expose the behavior of the system under invalid input, malformed states, or induced failures. These tests should assert that error messages are accurate and that fallback or retry mechanisms trigger correctly.

In automated test suites, employing an explicit enumeration of error scenarios, coupled with expected outcomes, provides a strong baseline:

```
def test_open_file_error_handling(monkeypatch):
    def fake_open(*args, **kwargs):
        raise IOError("Simulated I/O error")
    monkeypatch.setattr("builtins.open", fake_open)

    with pytest.raises(IOError) as excinfo:
        config = read_config_file("nonexistent.cfg")
    assert "Simulated I/O error" in str(excinfo.value)
```

This approach validates that error exceptions not only arise but also carry correct diagnostic information.

Integrating error condition tests with continuous integration (CI) systems ensures regression prevention and promotes early defect detection. Tests designed for error paths must be:

- **Deterministic and Repeatable**: Ensuring simulation settings are stable avoids flaky failures.

- **Isolated and Idempotent**: Each test should clean up after execution to avoid cross-test contamination, which is critical when simulating error states like resource exhaustion.

- **Comprehensive Coverage**: Utilizing coverage tools can highlight rarely hit error code paths, guiding expansion of test cases.

This ongoing validation improves confidence that error handling remains effective under evolving codebase changes.

Testing error conditions requires a multifaceted approach emphasizing proactive fault simulation and thorough correctness checks:

- Employ assertions where appropriate during development to catch erroneous assumptions.

- Use mocks, fault injection, and controlled overrides to simulate diverse error scenarios.

- Verify error propagation integrity, resource correctness, and state consistency after error handling.

- Design negative tests that assert both triggers and outcomes of failure conditions.

- Automate these tests within CI pipelines, ensuring repeatability and consistent coverage.

Without rigorous testing of error paths, software risks hidden faults that manifest under adverse conditions, potentially causing severe failures. Diligent application of these methodologies fortifies system robustness and reliability, crucial traits in advanced technology applications.

Chapter 8

Go Toolchain and Build System

Go's seamless tooling is as much a triumph as its language design. In this chapter, uncover how Go's sophisticated build system, dependency management, and developer tools underpin fast iteration, reliable delivery, and code quality at scale. Learn why the Go toolchain is admired for making robust builds feel effortless— and how it can amplify your own development workflow.

8.1. Go Modules and Dependency Management

The introduction of Go modules represents a pivotal advancement in the management of dependencies, modularity, and reproducibility within the Go ecosystem. Prior to Go modules, dependency management relied heavily on GOPATH and third-party tools, creating challenges related to version conflicts, reproducibility, and project portability. Modules provide a first-class mechanism that incorporates versioning, dependency resolution, and reproducible

181

builds, making contemporary Go development more robust and scalable.

At the core of Go modules lies the `go.mod` file, which defines the module's path and its required dependencies along with their minimum versions. The module path typically corresponds to a repository location, such as `github.com/user/project`, thereby uniquely identifying the module in version control systems and the broader Go ecosystem. An example `go.mod` file appears as follows:

```
module github.com/example/project

go 1.20

require (
    github.com/sirupsen/logrus v1.9.0
    golang.org/x/net v0.7.0
)
```

The `go 1.20` directive specifies the Go language version syntax compatibility. The `require` block introduces explicit dependency versioning, which facilitates deterministic builds by freezing all transitive state necessary for compilation.

Modules enable semantic import versioning through the use of major suffixes in module paths-for example, `github.com/example/project/v2`-to differentiate incompatible API versions. This mechanism allows multiple major versions of a dependency to coexist in the same build graph without ambiguity, adhering to the principles of semantic versioning (semver). The Go toolchain automatically interprets and enforces these version constraints during dependency resolution.

Dependency resolution operates through the go command, which consults the `go.mod` file, downloads missing modules from proxies or version control systems, and records exact module versions in a companion file named `go.sum`. This checksum file guarantees the integrity and authenticity of module content, mitigating supply chain risks:

```
github.com/sirupsen/logrus v1.9.0 h1:kP3+DkBj4W3/NwEpLf+
```

```
    xxGz9EMjoRmUmcRf2SZQNvQM=
github.com/sirupsen/logrus v1.9.0/go.mod h1:9
    gVBWbks1KXL2fJTZE6rSHQCnSjezWOq9pS46hP+1W8=
```

By coupling go.mod and go.sum, Go achieves immutable dependencies, ensuring that builds are fully reproducible and insulated from external changes or accidental updates.

Vendoring represents an alternative or complementary technique to providing reproducible builds by copying a project's dependencies into a local vendor directory. Running

```
go mod vendor
```

populates the vendor folder with the exact source code of all required dependencies as specified in the go.mod file. This approach enables projects to be built entirely offline and avoids reliance on external module proxies or repositories. The Go compiler and linker automatically prioritize packages found in the vendor directory when this mechanism is in use, guaranteeing consistency in builds.

While vendoring can increase repository size, it remains indispensable in corporate or air-gapped environments where external network access is restricted. Best practice involves careful version control and periodic go mod tidy operations to keep dependencies clean and minimal. This command prunes unused dependencies and updates go.mod and go.sum accordingly.

Project organization following modular principles significantly enhances maintainability and scalability. Key recommendations include defining clear module boundaries aligned with functional or domain-specific areas and maintaining stable API surfaces across versions. Splitting large monoliths into multiple modules enables independent versioning and reduces clutter in dependency graphs.

Complex projects may benefit from a hierarchical module structure. For instance, a root module github.com/org/project can depend on submodules such as github.com/org/project/pkgA

183

and `github.com/org/project/pkgB`, each with their own `go.mod` files. This subdivision caters to fine-grained dependency control and simplifies version upgrades or rollbacks.

To avoid common pitfalls, developers should:

- Keep `go.mod` files at the root of each module, avoiding mixing module files and source code ambiguities.

- Use semantic versioning consistently, incrementing major versions only for backward-incompatible changes.

- Commit both `go.mod` and `go.sum` files to version control to lock in dependencies and checksums.

- Leverage `go mod tidy` regularly to remove stale dependencies, improve build speed, and reduce security risks.

- Understand the interplay between vendoring and module proxies, deciding on a case-by-case basis what strategy best fits the environment.

Go modules provide a comprehensive system for dependency and version management, enabling reproducible builds and supporting modular codebases. Mastery of `go.mod` semantics, vendoring, and module organization is essential for maintaining healthy, scalable, and secure projects as the code base and team size grow.

8.2. Building, Installing, and Running

The go tool serves as the central command for compiling, installing, and executing Go programs, streamlining the software development process with a consistent interface. Mastering its invocation is essential for efficient development and deployment of Go applications.

The fundamental command for building a Go program is `go build`. This command compiles the packages named by the import paths, along with their dependencies, but it does not install the results into the workspace. By default, when executed in a directory containing a main package, `go build` produces an executable binary in the current directory named after the directory. For example, in a directory `hello`, with a `main.go` implementing `package main`, running

```
go build
```

produces an executable `hello` (or `hello.exe` on Windows). No installation occurs; the binary remains local to the working directory.

The `go install` command is used to compile and install packages and commands. When run on command packages, `go install` compiles and places the resulting executable into the `$GOPATH/bin` (or `$GOBIN` if set) directory, which should be included in the user's `PATH` for convenient invocation. This separation between building and installing encourages a development cycle where frequent builds check correctness and behavior locally, while `go install` prepares binaries explicitly for distribution or deployment.

Running a Go program can be streamlined with the `go run` command, which compiles and immediately executes the specified source files, bypassing a manual build step:

```
go run main.go
```

This is convenient for rapid iteration, particularly for small scripts or prototypes, though it is less efficient for larger programs requiring repeated tests due to repeated compilation.

Build Modes

The `go build` command supports various build modes, controlled via the `-buildmode` flag, to tailor the output binary for different use cases. Common build modes include:

- `exe`: The default mode, building a standalone executable.

- `c-shared`: Produces a shared library (.so or .dll) exposing Go functions that can be called from C programs.

- `c-archive`: Produces a static archive (.a) along with a C header, permitting embedding Go code in C applications.

- `pie`: Builds a position-independent executable, useful for systems enforcing address space layout randomization.

- `shared`: Builds shared libraries for Go packages to be linked dynamically.

These modes enable Go programs to interoperate smoothly with other languages, support dynamic linking, and meet platform-specific deployment requirements. Selection of the appropriate build mode depends on the target environment and integration needs.

Output Binary Structure

Go binaries produced by the `go build` tool are statically linked by default, incorporating the Go runtime, garbage collector, internal libraries, and all dependencies into a single executable. This reduces runtime dependencies, facilitating portability and simplifying deployment. Unlike traditional dynamically linked executables, Go binaries typically do not rely on external shared libraries for functionality except for system calls provided by the operating system.

Internally, Go binaries have a structure optimized for the runtime. The executable includes:

- A header with platform-specific metadata.

- Sections containing compiled machine code.

- Embedded symbol tables and debugging information.

- Static data segments for global variables.

- The Go runtime, including goroutine schedulers, garbage collection logic, and internal helper functions.

Because the runtime and standard libraries are linked in, Go executables can be relatively large compared to minimalist C counterparts, but this trade-off ensures fast startup times and robust concurrency support without external dependencies.

Streamlined Development Loop

The Go toolchain facilitates an efficient development loop through fast compilation and straightforward execution commands. Typical workflows involve the following iterations:

- Edit source files in the workspace or module.

- Run go build to check for compilation errors and to produce updated binaries.

- Execute the binary directly or with go run during exploratory development.

- When ready to deploy or share, use go install to place the binary in the user's bin directory.

Incremental compiling is implicitly supported through package caching. When a package is built, its compiled object is cached in $GOPATH/pkg or module cache directories. Subsequent builds reuse this cached data if the source and dependencies have not changed, dramatically improving build speeds for medium and large projects.

Build tags and environment variables such as GOOS and GOARCH extend the build process, allowing developers to produce binaries targeting different operating systems and processor architectures with a single command:

```
GOOS=linux GOARCH=amd64 go build -o myprog-linux
```

This capability is integral to cross-compilation workflows, removing the need for separate build environments.

Through this combination of simple commands, flexible build modes, and embedded runtime characteristics, the Go toolchain empowers developers to maintain a rapid feedback cycle from code change to execution, while ensuring that binaries are robust, portable, and ready for deployment in complex production contexts.

8.3. Package Visibility and Internal Packages

Go's approach to package visibility and encapsulation is deliberately minimalist yet potent, emphasizing simplicity and uniformity in the management of symbol visibility across compilation units. Visibility rules in Go are governed primarily by identifier naming conventions rather than explicit access modifiers found in other languages, such as `private` or `public`. This simplicity streamlines both code writing and comprehension but also allows nuanced control mechanisms through package structuring and directory conventions.

Identifiers in Go are exported (i.e., visible outside their package) if and only if they begin with an uppercase letter. Conversely, identifiers starting with a lowercase letter are unexported and restricted in visibility to the package in which they are declared. This behavior applies uniformly to all types of package-level declarations: functions, variables, constants, types, and methods. For example, a function named `Foo` in package `bar` will be accessible as `bar.Foo` from other packages, whereas `foo` remains private.

This implicit visibility by identifier casing sets the foundation for encapsulation but does not by itself provide access control granularity finer than the package boundary. To achieve stronger encapsulation, Go programmers often leverage the package and directory layout conventions that the Go tooling enforces. Notably, the *internal package* convention plays a critical role here.

An `internal` package is any package placed within a directory named `internal` inside a module or repository. The Go compiler enforces a strict visibility rule: packages outside the tree rooted at the parent of the `internal` directory cannot import any packages contained within. For instance, consider the directory hierarchy:

```
myproject/
  pkg/
    util/
  internal/
    crypt/
```

Packages outside `myproject` cannot import `internal/crypt`, effectively making it inaccessible externally despite containing exported identifiers. This convention introduces an enforcement mechanism that package-level visibility alone cannot provide, enabling repositories and modules to delimit a slice of code as strictly private to their internal implementation.

The enforcement of the `internal` directory constraint relies on the module or repository root's directory structure. Tools such as `go build` and `go list` verify import paths and disallow any imports outside the permitted subtree. This stands in contrast to regular package visibility, which relies solely on identifier case.

Besides the `internal` package mechanism, Go also formalizes vendoring as an approach for component encapsulation and reproducible builds. Vendoring involves committing the dependencies used by a module within a dedicated `vendor` directory inside the project root. The Go tooling gives preferential import resolution to packages found in this `vendor` directory, thus isolating dependencies from changes in remote repositories and external code.

Conceptually, vendoring can be viewed as a coarse-grained encapsulation strategy: by vendoring, a project creates a private snapshot of its dependencies, including their internal packages, which remain inaccessible to external code unless explicitly exposed through the public API surface. Vendored dependencies behave according to their original package visibility rules but operate as a self-contained subtree, mitigating potential disruptions from external code evolution.

Combining identifier-based visibility, `internal` packages, and vendoring permits Go programmers to finely control component exposure:

- Unexported identifiers enforce encapsulation within a package.

- `internal` packages restrict import scope to a subtree of the project, preventing external dependency leakage.

- Vendoring guarantees the stability and isolation of dependencies, preserving encapsulation guarantees even when external sources are mutable.

It is significant to note that while access control and encapsulation in Go are modest compared to languages that offer explicit keywords for these properties, Go's philosophy favors simplicity and transparency. Developers are encouraged to organize code thoughtfully into packages, utilizing naming conventions and directory structures as the primary tools to achieve modular design and maintain encapsulation.

The usage of `internal` packages also complements Go's tooling and ecosystem. Tools like `go doc` and language servers respect these boundaries and avoid exposing internal symbols unnecessarily. Additionally, internal packages are especially useful for large projects and libraries: implementation details can be sequestered in internal packages, enabling a clear API boundary and reducing coupling in client code.

Go's rules for package visibility combine straightforward syntax-level export criteria with deliberate directory layout conventions to enforce encapsulation boundaries. Internal packages restrict visibility beyond package-level unexported identifiers, providing a mechanism for internal modularization within a repository or module. Vendoring supplements these by encapsulating dependency code within a project's control. Together, these mechanisms enable robust, maintainable component design aligned with Go's principles of simplicity and clarity in package structure and visibility control.

8.4. Testing, Benchmarking, and Coverage

Go provides a comprehensive set of built-in tools that facilitate rigorous testing, benchmarking, fuzzing, and code coverage analysis, all integral to maintaining high-quality, maintainable software. The cornerstone of Go's testing infrastructure is the testing package, which supports idiomatic test discovery, execution, and reporting mechanisms.

Testing in Go relies on naming conventions that the go test command uses to automatically discover test functions. A test function must be exported, reside in a _test.go file, and have the signature:

```
func TestXxx(t *testing.T) { ... }
```

where Xxx can be any alphanumeric string beginning with an uppercase letter. This discovery mechanism allows seamless integration of tests across packages without requiring explicit registration. The *testing.T parameter provides methods such as Error, Fail, and Fatal to indicate test failures. To group related tests, developers often use table-driven tests, which promote modularity and scalability by iterating over a slice of test cases:

```
func TestCompute(t *testing.T) {
    tests := []struct {
        input  int
        output int
```

191

```
}{
    {1, 2},
    {2, 4},
}
for _, tc := range tests {
    t.Run(fmt.Sprintf("Input%d", tc.input), func(t *testing.T
    ) {
        got := Compute(tc.input)
        if got != tc.output {
            t.Errorf("Compute(%d) = %d; want %d", tc.input,
got, tc.output)
        }
    })
}
}
```

The use of t.Run spawns subtests, facilitating fine-grained control and reporting, and supports parallel execution when coupled with t.Parallel().

Benchmarking harnesses the testing package similarly, with functions conforming to:

```
func BenchmarkXxx(b *testing.B) { ... }
```

Here, the *testing.B type includes the integer field N which controls the number of iterations. Benchmarks must be designed to execute the tested code N times to yield statistically significant results. For example:

```
func BenchmarkSortInts(b *testing.B) {
    data := rand.Perm(1000)
    b.ResetTimer()
    for i := 0; i < b.N; i++ {
        slice := make([]int, len(data))
        copy(slice, data)
        sort.Ints(slice)
    }
}
```

The call to b.ResetTimer() ensures that setup time is excluded from the benchmark timing. Benchmark outputs include nanoseconds per operation and can be enhanced with custom metrics or memory allocations by invoking b.ReportAllocs().

Go 1.18 introduced native fuzzing support integrated directly into the testing package. Fuzz tests share a naming convention similar to unit tests but with FuzzXxx signatures:

```
func FuzzParseURL(f *testing.F) { ... }
```

Initial seed inputs are added via f.Add(...). The fuzzing engine automatically generates and mutates inputs to explore edge cases that could induce unexpected behavior or panics. When a crash or unexpected output is detected, the input corpus is minimized to a minimal reproducing test case, facilitating debugging.

Code coverage analysis can be enabled through the go test tool using the -cover flag, which instruments the code under test to track statement execution. Running

```
go test -cover ./...
```

produces a summary coverage percentage. For detailed reporting, -coverprofile generates a file that can be analyzed with go tool cover:

```
go test -coverprofile=coverage.out ./...
go tool cover -html=coverage.out
```

This renders an annotated HTML view showing which lines were executed and which were not, providing visual insight to guide test improvements. Coverage thresholds can be enforced in continuous integration pipelines by parsing coverage outputs, effectively preventing regressions in test suite completeness.

Maintaining robust test suites in Go involves a combination of idiomatic patterns and continuous practices. Table-driven tests and subtests enhance modularity and readability, making it easier to extend coverage as features evolve. Benchmarks should be updated alongside code changes to detect performance regressions early. Fuzz testing complements traditional tests by targeting input validation and error handling paths, an area often overlooked in manual test design.

193

Seamless integration with go test tooling encourages frequent execution of tests and benchmarks. Developers often script make commands or use go generate hooks to automate test runs and coverage reporting. Code reviews enforce thoroughness of tests, emphasizing edge case coverage, error conditions, and race detection (go test -race).

Instrumenting tests for concurrency correctness is particularly critical in Go, as goroutine scheduling can expose nondeterministic bugs. Parallel subtests and testing.T.Parallel() aid in simulating real-world concurrency, while race detector support helps uncover data races.

Go's built-in tooling leverages conventions and tightly integrated language features to make testing, benchmarking, fuzzing, and coverage analysis a natural extension of development workflows. This synergy supports the evolution of large-scale, high-performance codebases with confidence in correctness, efficiency, and robustness over time.

8.5. Static Analysis and Code Formatting

The Go programming language ecosystem is distinguished by a robust collection of tools focused on static analysis and automated code formatting. These tools not only detect potential errors and enforce coding standards but also cultivate a consistent style across diverse development teams, thereby enhancing maintainability and productivity.

Central to Go's approach to static analysis is go vet, a tool that examines source code and reports suspicious constructs. Unlike traditional linters, which audit stylistic concerns, go vet performs semantic checks to uncover errors that compilers typically miss. For example, go vet identifies unreachable code, incorrect format verbs in Printf-style functions, and misuses of StructTag syntax.

Its analysis is based on an Abstract Syntax Tree (AST) and takes type information into account, enabling detection of subtle bugs:

- Incorrect argument counts in formatted I/O calls.

- Calls to `reflect.TypeOf` on unaddressable variables.

- Composite literal constructions with duplicate keys.

go vet is integrated into Go's build and test workflows and can be invoked manually:

```
go vet ./...
```

This command exhaustively analyzes the entire module directory tree, surfacing potential defects before runtime. Its adoption is widely recommended as a standard quality gate.

Complementing go vet are community-supported linters, such as those bundled in the `golangci-lint` aggregator. These tools perform stylistic and correctness checks extending beyond go vet's scope. For instance, linters identify unused variables, missing error checks, cyclomatic complexity thresholds, and code smells that may impede readability or robustness. The composite nature of `golangci-lint` allows parallel execution of multiple linters with a single command:

```
golangci-lint run
```

By applying such linters early and continuously, teams reduce technical debt and enforce best practices systematically.

Parallel to static analysis, Go emphasizes automated code formatting to enforce uniformity. The `gofmt` utility is a hallmark tool that parses Go source files and rewrites them to adhere to a canonical style. This process removes subjective formatting debates, letting developers focus solely on logic and correctness. A typical invocation is:

```
gofmt -w main.go
```

which rewrites `main.go` in place. The formatting rules cover indentation, spacing, line breaks, and brace placement, all of which are standardized by `gofmt`'s internal parser.

Automatic formatting confers several critical benefits:

- **Code Consistency**: All code in a project appears homogeneous, improving readability across contributors.

- **Reduced Review Friction**: Code reviews can concentrate on semantic content rather than formatting nitpicks.

- **Integration with IDEs and Editors**: Many Go development environments invoke `gofmt` on save, ensuring seamless adherence to style guidelines.

Extending `gofmt`, `goimports` incorporates import statement management alongside formatting. It automatically adds missing package imports and removes unused ones while formatting the codebase, further streamlining development:

```
goimports -w main.go
```

The automated adjustment of import declarations is particularly advantageous in large codebases where manual maintenance of imports is error-prone and tedious.

Adoption of these tools is a cornerstone of professional Go programming. Incorporating automated formatting and static analysis into continuous integration pipelines enforces a consistent quality baseline. The enforcement is not optional; rather, it is a fundamental aspect of Go projects' culture. Developers encountering `go vet` errors or formatting diffs are compelled to correct them promptly due to the tooling integration with version control systems and code review bots.

The consequence of such strict enforcement translates directly into team productivity. When all members produce code that meets the same stylistic and correctness criteria, cognitive overhead during peer review and debugging diminishes significantly. Clear, predictable code formatting reduces mental load by allowing developers to focus on program logic rather than deciphering unstructured code. Moreover, static analysis tools catch defects early in the development cycle, minimizing costly bug fixes and regressions downstream.

Go's suite of static analysis and formatting tools forms an ecosystem that enforces best practices effortlessly and uniformly. `go vet` provides semantic correctness checks, while `gofmt` and `goimports` guarantee standardized formatting and import hygiene. These enforceable conventions cultivate maintainable, high-quality codebases that scale well across teams, setting a high bar for software craftsmanship in Go environments.

8.6. Cross Compilation and Build Constraints

Go's design philosophy embraces simplicity and portability, offering a straightforward cross-compilation mechanism that enables the creation of binaries for multiple operating systems and architectures from a single development environment. This capability is tightly integrated with the language's build system and drastically reduces the complexity traditionally associated with cross-platform development.

Go Cross-Compilation Model

Cross compilation in Go is primarily achieved through environment variables that control the target platform. The two principal variables are `GOOS` (target operating system) and `GOARCH` (target architecture). Setting these before invoking the `go build` command instructs the compiler and linker to produce binaries tailored for the specified platform, independent of the host environment.

```
GOOS=windows GOARCH=amd64 go build -o program.exe
```

The toolchain supports a broad range of GOOS values, including linux, darwin (macOS), windows, freebsd, and others. Likewise, GOARCH supports architectures like amd64, 386, arm, arm64, and ppc64le. The process handles system call differences, runtime linking, and architecture-specific optimizations intrinsically, producing statically linked binaries where feasible.

Build Constraints and Tags

Build constraints (also called build tags) control the inclusion or exclusion of files or code segments based on the target platform, compiler version, or custom-defined tags. They are specified as Boolean expressions in comments at the top of Go source files. A canonical constraint appears as:

```
//go:build linux && amd64
// +build linux,amd64
```

These lines specify that the file compiles only when both linux OS and amd64 architecture are targeted. The newer //go:build syntax is preferred in modern Go versions due to improved readability and tooling support, but both forms ensure backward compatibility.

Build constraints can specify logical operations && (AND), || (OR), and ! (NOT), enabling complex conditional compilation scenarios. The build system evaluates these expressions to include appropriate files and exclude irrelevant ones automatically.

File Naming Conventions

Complementing build tags, Go relies on filename suffixes to apply platform constraints. These suffixes serve as implicit build constraints and follow the pattern _GOOS or _GOARCH before the file extension. For example, a file named network_linux.go is compiled only when targeting Linux; handler_amd64.go compiles only when targeting the AMD64 architecture. This convention allows developers to organize platform-specific implementations cleanly without verbose build tags.

Selective Compilation Within Files

Beyond file-level constraints, conditional compilation can be refined to the function or statement level through custom build tags combined with build flags or runtime checks. Although Go does not support a preprocessor like #ifdef in C, the idiomatic approach is to separate platform-specific code into distinct files with appropriate build constraints, thus encouraging a clean separation of concerns.

An alternative approach uses the build tag in conjunction with the //go:build directive:

```
//go:build darwin || linux

package main

func platformSpecificFunction() {
    // Implementation for Unix-like OSes
}
```

Files without build constraints are treated as universal and included for all target platforms.

Custom Build Tags

Custom build tags empower developers to introduce compilation conditions beyond system-level constraints. These are defined by the user and specified at build time using the -tags flag:

```
go build -tags=container
```

Within source files, the tag is referenced through a build constraint comment:

```
//go:build container
// +build container
```

This facility is invaluable for toggling features, enabling experimental APIs, or splitting debug and release builds without extensively modifying build scripts or environment variables.

Implications for Library and CLI Development

Cross-compilation and build constraints in Go are particularly advantageous when developing libraries and command-line interfaces intended to run seamlessly across diverse environments. Libraries can conditionally expose platform-specific optimizations while preserving a consistent API surface. CLI tools benefit from single-source code bases capable of supplying native binaries for multiple platforms, simplifying distribution and deployment.

Handling Cgo and External Dependencies

When cross-compiling, the presence of `cgo` (C interoperability) introduces complexity because the Go compiler relies on the host toolchain's cross-compilers for non-Go code. To facilitate cross compilation with `cgo`, developers must ensure the availability of appropriate cross compilers for the target platform and correctly set `CC` and related environment variables. Alternatively, disabling `cgo` by setting `CGO_ENABLED=0` allows generating fully static binaries without external dependencies, although some system-specific or low-level features may be inaccessible.

Example: Cross-Compilation Workflow

Consider building a cross-platform command-line utility supporting Linux, macOS, and Windows on both amd64 and arm64 architectures. The developer would:

- Organize source files using platform-specific suffixes such as `file_linux.go`, `file_windows.go`.

- Utilize build tags to isolate platform-specific implementations not easily separable by file naming.

- Cross-compile binaries using shell scripts or Makefiles setting `GOOS` and `GOARCH` accordingly.

- Use the `-tags` flag to enable optional features or debug modes.

```
GOOS=darwin    GOARCH=arm64  go build -o tool_darwin_arm64
GOOS=windows   GOARCH=amd64  go build -o tool_windows_amd64.exe
GOOS=linux     GOARCH=amd64  go build -o tool_linux_amd64
```

Each binary is optimized and compatible with its target platform, having included only the necessary platform-specific code during compilation.

Key practices include:

- Setting GOOS and GOARCH environment variables to determine target platform and architecture.

- Using build constraints (//go:build and +build) to conditionally compile source files.

- Leveraging filename suffixes for implicit platform filtering.

- Defining and applying custom build tags to control feature sets or build variants.

- Managing cgo dependencies carefully when cross-compiling; considering disabling cgo if possible.

- Structuring the codebase with clear separation between platform-agnostic and platform-specific components.

This combination of robust, declarative cross-compilation and flexible build constraints ensures that Go programs can efficiently adapt to the requirements of diverse system environments while maintaining a clear, maintainable source structure.

Chapter 9

Advanced Language Features and Runtime Aspects

Go's elegance belies remarkable depth—from generics and reflection to seamless foreign integration and runtime diagnostics. This chapter unlocks Go's most sophisticated features, showing how the language empowers high-performance systems, safe extensibility, and evolution without compromise. Discover the hidden levers that give Go its adaptability for modern, production-grade software.

9.1. Generics and Type Parameters

Go's introduction of generics in version 1.18 marked a fundamental advance in the language's capacity for abstraction and type safety. Generics enable the definition of functions, types, and data structures that operate across a variety of underlying types while preserving static type checks. This section examines the syntax of generics in Go, the nature of type constraints, and their practical applications for crafting safer and reusable abstractions. It further discusses the benefits and trade-offs, providing guidance for when generics should be employed in software design.

At the core of Go's generics is the concept of type parameters, which are specified in square brackets directly after the identifier of a function or type. Type parameters are declared with an associated constraint, ensuring that only types meeting certain conditions are permitted. The simplest form of a type parameter declaration is:

```
func Identity[T any](value T) T {
    return value
}
```

Here, T is a type parameter constrained by the predeclared constraint any, which accepts all types. The function Identity returns the input value exactly, serving as a canonical example of parametric polymorphism.

Constraints in Go generics serve as compile-time predicates on type parameters, limiting permissible types. The any constraint is an alias for interface{}, indicating no restrictions, but more commonly, developers use interfaces that specify required methods or type sets. For example:

```
type Comparable interface {
    ~int | ~float64 | ~string
}

func Max[T Comparable](a, b T) T {
    if a > b {
        return a
    }
    return b
}
```

This code defines a Comparable constraint as a union of underlying types supporting the > operator through structuring with tilde (~), which designates approximation to these base types. The Max function finds the maximum of two comparable values, ensuring compile-time enforcement that the types used support comparison operations. Without generics, it would require distinct functions per type or the use of interface{} with runtime type assertions and loss of static safety.

Type constraints can also specify interface method sets, such as collections supporting Len and Less:

```
type Ordered interface {
    Less(other Ordered) bool
}

type Sortable[T Ordered] []T

func (s Sortable[T]) Len() int {
    return len(s)
}

func (s Sortable[T]) Less(i, j int) bool {
    return s[i].Less(s[j])
}
```

This leverages generics to define a sortable collection that can work uniformly with any type implementing the Ordered interface. Embedding behavior in constraints allows rich, reusable abstractions without sacrificing safety or performance.

Generics enable writing generic data structure implementations, eliminating repetitive boilerplate due to language limitation on type specification. For example, a generic singly linked list can be created as:

```
type Node[T any] struct {
    Value T
    Next  *Node[T]
}

type LinkedList[T any] struct {
    Head *Node[T]
}

func (list *LinkedList[T]) Append(value T) {
    newNode := &Node[T]{Value: value}
    if list.Head == nil {
        list.Head = newNode
```

```
        return
    }
    current := list.Head
    for current.Next != nil {
        current = current.Next
    }
    current.Next = newNode
}
```

This approach encapsulates data structure logic once while supporting arbitrary element types. The advantages over using interface{} include no requirement for type assertions on retrieval and greater runtime efficiency via compile-time type resolution.

However, the introduction of generics carries certain trade-offs. Generics often increase code complexity and can reduce readability when overused, especially for developers unfamiliar with parametric polymorphism. Moreover, while Go's generics are designed to avoid runtime overhead, their implementation can cause increased binary sizes and compile times, particularly in large codebases with deeply nested or heavily generic code.

Generics are most appropriate in cases involving data structures, algorithms, and utilities that operate identically across multiple types, such as sorting, searching, or container libraries. Conversely, for specialized behavior tightly coupled to specific types or where runtime reflection-based polymorphism is acceptable, traditional interfaces without generics may suffice. Designing with generics requires balancing abstraction with simplicity and considering the maintenance impact on a development team.

Go's generics provide a powerful toolset for safer, reusable abstractions by parametrizing code with type parameters and enforcing constraints at compile time. This facilitates polymorphic functions and data structures without compromising Go's trademark simplicity and performance. Skilled application of generics leads to cleaner, more maintainable code with fewer runtime type errors, though their usage should be calibrated carefully against code complexity and build considerations.

9.2. The Go Runtime and Garbage Collection

The Go runtime is a fundamental component that orchestrates execution, resource management, and scheduling within Go applications. Central to its functionality are three major aspects: memory management, goroutine scheduling, and garbage collection (GC). A comprehensive understanding of these facets is essential for optimizing performance, especially in demanding, concurrency-heavy environments.

At its core, memory management in Go involves automatic allocation and reclamation of heap-allocated objects. Unlike many languages that rely on explicit memory management, Go employs a concurrent, non-generational garbage collector which integrates smoothly with goroutine scheduling. Memory allocation requests are served by the runtime's allocator, which uses thread-local allocators-known as *mcaches*-attached to each operating system (OS) thread (also called a P in the Go runtime terminology) to reduce contention in multithreaded scenarios.

The allocator manages memory in spans, contiguous regions of physical pages, which are carved into objects of uniform size categorized by size classes. Small objects (up to 32 KB) are allocated from these span caches, while larger objects receive whole spans or multiple spans. This organization enables efficient allocation and helps reduce fragmentation. Returning memory to the OS is handled conservatively to balance performance benefits against memory footprint, minimized through mechanisms like scavenging.

Goroutine scheduling within the runtime is another critical factor affecting application responsiveness and throughput. Go utilizes a hybrid M:N scheduler model, where M OS threads multiplex N goroutines. Each OS thread is bound to a processor context (P), and each *P* holds a local run queue of runnable goroutines. The scheduler balances load among *P*s by work-stealing to avoid starvation. Preemption is cooperative but has been progressively enhanced to include asynchronous preemption, improving latency guarantees for long-running goroutines.

The scheduler's design prioritizes low-overhead context switching and concurrency primitives that align closely with Go's `select` statement and synchronization types such as channels and mutexes. This synergy allows goroutines to appear lightweight, supporting the creation of millions of concurrent tasks without incurring the OS thread overhead.

Garbage collection, historically a source of overhead in many managed-language runtimes, is a pivotal aspect of the Go runtime, and its evolution warrants close attention. The current Go GC is a concurrent mark-and-sweep collector with a tri-color abstraction implemented through write barriers. Its operation divides into three phases:

1. **Mark initialization:** The GC prepares by scanning stacks and global roots for references to heap objects.

2. **Marking:** Concurrent workers trace live objects by following pointers, coloring objects grey or black in terms of their mark state while write barriers maintain consistency during mutator activity.

3. **Sweeping:** After marking, spans devoid of live objects are reclaimed and added back to free lists.

Importantly, the concurrent nature of the GC allows mutator goroutines to proceed with minimal stop-the-world pauses, which are currently in the low milliseconds scale for most workloads. The use of write barriers-code injected by the compiler to track pointer updates-ensures correctness without halting the entire program.

Tuning the Go runtime for applications with demanding latency or throughput constraints revolves around several parameters accessible through environment variables or programmatic interfaces:

- GOGC: This environment variable sets the target heap growth percentage triggering garbage collection. The default is 100 (meaning the heap can double in size before GC runs). Lowering GOGC trades higher GC frequency for reduced heap size, enhancing latency and memory pressure but increasing CPU overhead.

- GOMAXPROCS: Defines the maximum number of OS threads executing user-level Go code simultaneously, effectively tuning the parallelism of goroutine execution. Increasing GOMAXPROCS can improve throughput but also escalates contention and GC scheduling overhead.

- runtime/debug.SetGCPercent: Allows runtime adjustment of the GC target percentage, facilitating adaptive tuning within the application.

Profiling tools such as pprof, together with runtime tracing capabilities, are indispensable for understanding GC behavior, including pause times, allocation rates, and scheduler activity. The runtime/trace package provides granular traces that reveal goroutine states and GC cycles, enabling insightful diagnostics.

Advanced applications also benefit from controlling allocation patterns to assist the garbage collector. Techniques include:

- Minimizing large object allocations by reusing buffers with sync.Pool, which reduces pressure on the heap and limits GC scanning overhead.

- Avoiding pointer churning and promoting escape analysis to ensure objects remain on the stack where possible.

- Structuring data to reduce pointer relationships, enabling more effective compaction during GC.

Recent enhancements in Go 1.19 and later include background sweeping that occurs concurrently with marking, leading to smoother latencies. Additionally, the runtime uses proportional-integral-derivative (PID) feedback control to dynamically adjust GC pacing based on current mutator throughput, allowing adaptive balancing of pause time and CPU utilization.

In sum, the Go runtime embodies a sophisticated balance between efficient scheduling, low-overhead memory management, and a concurrent garbage collector tailored for scalable, high-concurrency applications. Mastery of its internals and tuning knobs is crucial for developers seeking to push Go programs beyond typical performance frontiers while maintaining predictable and manageable resource consumption.

9.3. Unsafe Operations and the unsafe Package

The unsafe package in Go provides a gateway to low-level programming by permitting operations that violate the language's usual type safety and memory safety guarantees. While the standard Go type system and memory management mechanisms are designed to prevent behaviors such as arbitrary memory access, type punning, and pointer arithmetic, the unsafe package explicitly enables these operations when necessary. This section explores the capabilities and inherent risks of using the unsafe package, elucidates when and why bypassing type safety might be justified, and outlines best practices for effective and secure low-level programming in Go.

The unsafe package exposes four primary features that facilitate unsafe programming:

- `unsafe.Pointer`: A special pointer type that can represent any arbitrary memory address without any type restrictions.

- `Sizeof`: Returns the size in bytes of a given variable or type.

- `Alignof`: Returns the alignment in bytes required for a given variable or type.

- `Offsetof`: Returns the offset in bytes of a field within a struct type.

These features collectively allow the programmer to manipulate memory layout, perform pointer arithmetic, and access struct fields at raw memory offsets, bypassing the compiler's usual checks for type correctness and memory safety.

For example, `unsafe.Pointer` enables conversions across unrelated pointer types, which is impossible with standard Go pointers. A common idiom to convert between pointer types is as follows:

```
var x int = 42
p := unsafe.Pointer(&x)
f := (*float64)(p)
```

Here, p stores the address of x as an `unsafe.Pointer`, and then it is reinterpreted as a pointer to a `float64`. This operation can be perilous if the memory representations differ, leading to undefined behavior.

Bypassing Go's type safety fundamentally undermines the compiler's and runtime's ability to guarantee program correctness and safety. The primary hazards involved include:

- **Memory Corruption**: Interpreting raw memory with incorrect types can lead to corrupted data structures, causing unpredictable program behavior.

- **Pointer Misuse**: Incorrect pointer arithmetic or conversions may violate memory boundaries, resulting in segmentation faults or data races.

- **Portability Issues**: Using unsafe assumes a particular memory layout and alignment, which can differ across architectures or compiler implementations.

- **Garbage Collector Confusion**: Conversions that obscure pointer types may prevent the garbage collector from correctly tracking references, causing premature memory reclamation or leaks.

For example, improperly casting a pointer and subsequently dereferencing it to a smaller or larger type than the original can overwrite adjacent memory, leading to memory corruption:

```
var i int64 = 0x0102030405060708
p := (*int32)(unsafe.Pointer(&i))
fmt.Printf("%#x\n", *p) // Outputs only the lower 4 bytes of i
```

Such code fragments may break if the underlying architecture or compiler changes packing or alignment rules.

Using the unsafe package is justified primarily in scenarios requiring fine-grained control over memory representation, performance optimizations, or interoperability with hardware or foreign code. Typical use cases include:

- **Optimizing Performance**: When eliminating redundant copies of data or avoiding expensive runtime checks can yield significant speedups, and the developer guarantees correctness by manual verification.

- **Interfacing with System Resources**: Accessing memory-mapped hardware registers, interacting with operating system internals, or integrating with C libraries often necessitates direct memory manipulation outside Go's normal abstractions.

- **Implementing Low-Level Data Structures**: Custom memory allocators, memory pools, or serialization routines may require precise control of memory layout and alignment.

However, these benefits come at the cost of complexity and fragility. Hence, employing unsafe should be accompanied by thorough understanding of underlying hardware, compiler behaviors, and Go's memory model.

To harness the power of unsafe without undermining program integrity, the following best practices are recommended:

- **Minimize Scope**: Confine unsafe operations to small, well-audited code segments. Avoid proliferating unsafe code throughout the project.

- **Encapsulate and Document**: Encapsulate unsafe operations within clearly defined functions or packages. Provide comprehensive documentation to explain assumptions and intended invariants.

- **Avoid Pointer Arithmetic Unless Necessary**: Use functions like Offsetof to calculate field positions instead of manual pointer arithmetic, ensuring correctness over iterations or platform changes.

- **Preserve Garbage Collector Safety**: When converting between pointers, ensure that Go pointers are not hidden from the garbage collector. For instance, convert pointers back and forth via unsafe.Pointer carefully, and never store unsafe pointers in Go pointer fields.

- **Use uintptr with Caution**: Recognize that uintptr is just an integer and garbage collector rules apply strictly; converting pointers to uintptr and back must be temporally confined to avoid collection or invalidation.

- **Align Data Properly**: Utilize Alignof to confirm alignment constraints of manipulated data types to prevent undefined behavior.

- **Prefer Standard Libraries**: When possible, use higher-level abstractions provided in the standard library or third-party packages that have safely wrapped unsafe operations.

For example, the safe use of unsafe to access raw bytes of a struct is often implemented as:

```
type Header struct {
    ID    uint32
    Flag byte
}

h := Header{ID: 1234, Flag: 1}
size := unsafe.Sizeof(h)
ptr := unsafe.Pointer(&h)
slice := (*[1 << 20]byte)(ptr)[:size:size] // Convert struct to
    byte slice
```

This pattern ensures that the size and alignment are explicitly respected, and the conversion remains consistent with the underlying data layout.

While unsafe provides unmatched control, it is inherently non-portable and error-prone. Developers should exhaust all safe alternatives, such as reflection, interfaces, or code generation before resorting to unsafe. Reflection, for instance, enables dynamic type inspection and manipulation with runtime checks, preserving safety at the cost of some overhead.

Additionally, Go's recent language enhancements and runtime optimizations have addressed many efficiency and interoperability concerns, further diminishing the need for unsafe constructs in day-to-day programming.

The unsafe package is a powerful tool for advanced Go programmers requiring direct memory management capabilities. Mastery of this package requires a deep understanding of type systems, memory layouts, and runtime implementation details. When wielded judiciously within disciplined practices, it enables performance optimizations and system-level integrations beyond the reach of conventional Go code, while any negligence risks critical system failures and undefined behaviors.

9.4. Cgo and Foreign Function Interfaces

Cross-language interoperability is a crucial capability when integrating software components that leverage specialized libraries or system-level functionalities unavailable in the native runtime environment. In the Go programming language, cgo provides a robust Foreign Function Interface (FFI) mechanism enabling integration with C libraries by bridging differences in memory layout, calling conventions, and data representations.

Memory Layout Considerations

C and Go employ distinct runtime models and memory management schemes, necessitating careful attention to the layout and ownership of data shared across language boundaries. Go uses a garbage-collected heap with pointer and type safety guarantees, while C relies on manual memory management and raw pointers.

When passing data structures from Go to C, it is critical to ensure that Go variables remain in memory and do not move during execution, as C expects stable pointers. This is achieved through using C.CBytes or allocating memory explicitly via C functions, and by leveraging unsafe.Pointer for type conversions. Conversely, pointers received from C must be converted carefully and not assumed to be managed by Go's garbage collector.

Byte arrays, structs, and pointers must mirror C's layout to avoid undefined behavior. The Go C package automatically generates Go struct definitions from C declarations to maintain field alignment and padding, but manual verification is often required for complex or platform-specific struct layouts.

Calling Conventions and Function Invocation

cgo abstracts the calling conventions, enabling seamless invocation of C functions as if they were native Go functions, with certain syntactic restrictions:

```
/*
#include <stdlib.h>
#include <string.h>

int add(int a, int b) {
    return a + b;
}
*/
import "C"
import "fmt"

func main() {
    res := C.add(10, 20)
    fmt.Println("Result:", int(res))
}
```

Here, the C.add function is callable directly. Parameters are implicitly converted according to their declared C types; however, complex types such as structs require explicit conversion between Go and C representations.

It is important to note the cost of calls across the FFI boundary, as each invocation may incur overhead related to stack switching, register saving, and calling convention adaptations. Batch processing or minimizing cross-boundary calls can significantly improve performance in latency-sensitive applications.

Memory Management in Interfacing

Properly managing memory lifecycle across Go and C is paramount to prevent leaks and undefined behavior. When C functions allocate memory (e.g., malloc), the Go code is responsible for calling the corresponding C deallocation functions (e.g., free) explicitly:

```
ptr := C.malloc(C.size_t(size))
// Use ptr ...
C.free(ptr)
```

Conversely, Go pointers must not be passed directly to C code unless pinned or converted to stable memory regions using C.CBytes or `runtime.KeepAlive`, guaranteeing that garbage collection does not relocate or free the underlying data during the C call.

Advanced Data Type Mapping

Primitive types such as `int`, `float`, and pointers have straightforward mappings: Go's `C.int` aligns with C's `int`, etc. However, composite and opaque types require more deliberate handling.

Structs

When passing structs, the Go definition must replicate the C struct's field order, alignment, and size. For example:

```
typedef struct {
    int x;
    double y;
} Point;
```

Translates to:

```
type Point C.Point
```

Manipulation of `Point` fields can occur either through type conversions or by unsafe pointer casting to maintain binary compatibility.

Strings

C strings are null-terminated byte arrays, while Go strings maintain length metadata and may contain embedded zeros. Passing Go strings to C requires conversion using `C.CString`, which allocates C heap memory for the string and must be freed after use:

```
cs := C.CString(goStr)
defer C.free(unsafe.Pointer(cs))
// Pass cs to C functions
```

Returning C strings to Go requires creating Go strings via `C.GoString` with care to manage ownership and lifetime.

Real-World Integration Scenarios

System Calls and Low-Level APIs

When leveraging OS-level APIs or hardware libraries implemented in C, cgo serves as an indispensable tool to write Go wrappers that provide type-safe, idiomatic interfaces. For instance, around POSIX socket APIs or specialized hardware drivers, cgo enables invoking system calls unavailable natively in Go's standard library.

Third-Party Libraries

Popular libraries for cryptography, image processing, or scientific computing often expose C APIs. Integrating these via cgo allows reusing battle-tested implementations without rewriting in Go, thus embracing hybrid architectures for optimized throughput and reliability.

Performance-Critical Components

Complex computations or latency-sensitive code benefiting from hand-tuned C implementations can be called from Go. Developers are advised to encapsulate these calls into small interfaces, manage data marshaling efficiently, and minimize cross-boundary invocations to achieve performance goals.

Best Practices for Safe and Efficient Integration

- **Minimize Calls Across the Boundary:** Group operations in C where possible to reduce call overhead.

- **Explicit Memory Ownership:** Clearly document and follow conventions for which side owns allocated memory and who must free it.

- **Use Go Wrappers:** Encapsulate cgo calls within idiomatic Go packages, hiding unsafe or complex operations behind safe abstractions.

- **Avoid Passing Go Pointers to C:** Unless using cgo rules and runtime mechanisms to pin data, passing Go pointers leads to subtle memory errors.

- **Check Platform Compatibility:** Different architectures may vary in data alignment and calling conventions; conditional compilation and thorough testing are recommended.

- **Profile and Benchmark:** Measure the cost of FFI calls under real workloads to identify bottlenecks, and optimize data formats and invocation patterns accordingly.

Error Handling Across Languages

Error reporting conventions in C often involve return codes or global variables such as errno, whereas Go uses explicit error values. Bridging these systems requires manual translation, for example:

```
ret := C.some_function()
if ret != 0 {
    err := fmt.Errorf("C function failed with code %d", int(ret))
    return err
}
```

Additional wrappers can translate common error codes into Go error types for idiomatic handling.

Limitations and Alternatives

While cgo is powerful, it introduces build complexities, increases binary size, and complicates cross-compilation. For certain applications, other methods such as RPC, shared libraries invoked via syscall, or embedding scripting languages may be preferable.

Nonetheless, for scenarios demanding tight integration with C runtime libraries or system APIs, cgo remains the most direct and efficient FFI approach within the Go ecosystem.

Proper mastery of cgo is essential for developers aiming to combine Go's strengths in concurrency and safety with the vast ecosystem of existing C libraries, enabling the construction of performant and feature-rich software systems.

9.5. Reflection: Advanced Patterns

Reflection furnishes the capacity to inspect and manipulate program structures dynamically at runtime, thereby enabling advanced programming patterns that transcend static code limitations. These patterns, when leveraged judiciously, facilitate the automated generation of codecs, development of flexible serialization frameworks, and creation of dynamic application programming interfaces (APIs). However, the profound power embedded in reflection also introduces layers of complexity related to performance, security, and maintainability, demanding thorough understanding and careful implementation.

At the core of many reflection-driven frameworks lies the automatic generation of codecs-systems for encoding and decoding data structures. By introspecting type metadata, constructors, and field properties, reflection allows dynamic derivation of serializers and deserializers without manual boilerplate code. Consider a typical approach in statically typed languages with runtime type information: a codec generator inspects a class's fields, extracts field names and types, and produces corresponding read and write routines.

An exemplary codec generation process involves recursively traversing the object graph to serialize nested objects. Reflection provides access to nested type descriptors, enabling generic codec construction on arbitrarily complex data types. This pattern both simplifies codebases by abstracting serialization logic and enhances extensibility by supporting new types without modifying serialization code directly. Below is a schematic pseudocode illustrating this pattern:

```
public Codec<?> generateCodec(Class<?> cls) {
    if (cls.isPrimitive() || cls == String.class) {
        return basicCodecFor(cls);
    }
    return new Codec<Object>() {
        public void encode(Object obj, OutputStream out) throws
    IOException {
```

```
        for (Field field : cls.getDeclaredFields()) {
            field.setAccessible(true);
            Object value = field.get(obj);
            Codec<?> codec = generateCodec(field.getType());
            codec.encode(value, out);
        }
    }

    public Object decode(InputStream in) throws IOException {
        Object instance = cls.getConstructor().newInstance();
        for (Field field : cls.getDeclaredFields()) {
            field.setAccessible(true);
            Codec<?> codec = generateCodec(field.getType());
            Object value = codec.decode(in);
            field.set(instance, value);
        }
        return instance;
    }
};
}
```

The generateCodec method above demonstrates dynamic codec creation by reflecting over fields and delegating encoding and decoding recursively. This pattern naturally generalizes to handle collections, maps, and polymorphic types by analyzing metadata and applying appropriate type-specific strategies.

Serialization frameworks extensively exploit such reflection capabilities to provide flexible, generic serialization without burdening developers with hand-crafted encoding logic for every custom type. Beyond mere field-oriented serialization, reflection supports advanced features such as version-tolerant serialization, where metadata guides conditional inclusion or transformation of fields depending on schema evolution. An annotation-driven model can further refine serialization behavior dynamically by embedding directives within type definitions, accessible via reflective APIs.

Dynamic APIs represent another frontier where reflection unlocks substantive capabilities. Typical use cases include creating proxies that forward method invocations to remote services, modifying object behaviors at runtime, or constructing API endpoints from metadata annotations automatically. For example, in web service frameworks, reflection reads controller class methods and generates HTTP handlers mapping method parameters and return types to request and response payloads dynamically.

This dynamism enables building adaptive, pluggable systems with APIs that evolve without recompilation or explicit configuration. Dynamic proxies created via reflection also support cross-cutting concerns such as logging, transaction management, and security by intercepting calls transparently. The proxy construction routinely involves generating invocation handlers that accept method invocation details, inspect method signatures and annotations, and apply suitable logic, as shown:

```
InvocationHandler handler = new InvocationHandler() {
    public Object invoke(Object proxy, Method method, Object[]
    args) throws Throwable {
        if (method.isAnnotationPresent(Transactional.class)) {
            beginTransaction();
            try {
                Object result = method.invoke(target, args);
                commitTransaction();
                return result;
            } catch (Exception e) {
                rollbackTransaction();
                throw e;
            }
        }
        return method.invoke(target, args);
    }
};

Service proxyInstance = (Service) Proxy.newProxyInstance(
    Service.class.getClassLoader(),
    new Class<?>[] { Service.class },
    handler);
```

Although these patterns demonstrate reflection's unmatched flexibility, they also expose inherent complexities. Dynamic code paths obfuscate control flow, impairing readability and complicating debugging. The use of reflection incurs runtime overhead due to metadata extraction, method dispatch, and accessibility checks, which may degrade performance unless optimized. Furthermore, reflective code can circumvent static type checks, increasing susceptibility to runtime errors and security vulnerabilities if input is insufficiently validated.

To mitigate these risks, rigorous validation of reflective operations and cautious use of dynamic features are essential. Combining reflection with compile-time code generation or annotation processing can yield hybrid approaches that balance flexibility with safety and efficiency. For instance, generating serializers during compilation removes runtime penalties while preserving extensibility. Likewise, runtime reflection can be confined to initialization phases, minimizing impact during hot execution paths.

Reflection unlocks powerful advanced patterns essential for codec generation, adaptable serialization frameworks, and dynamic API construction. Mastery of these paradigms requires a keen appreciation for the delicate balance between expressiveness and the complexities introduced. Approaching reflection as a controlled tool-leveraged with strong typing disciplines, careful performance profiling, and robust error handling-enables developers to harness its benefits effectively and build resilient, maintainable software systems.

9.6. Monitoring, Profiling, and Diagnostics

Efficient management of Go applications in production environments entails a comprehensive understanding of runtime behavior. This requires leveraging robust tools for profiling, tracing, and diagnostics that illuminate execution flow, resource consumption, and performance bottlenecks. Go provides a rich ecosystem for such tasks, blending built-in capabilities with external utilities to facilitate fine-grained analysis and tuning.

Go's built-in `pprof` package is a cornerstone for capturing runtime profiles. It supports multiple profile types including CPU, memory (heap), goroutine blocking, and thread creation profiles. Profiling enables identification of the most CPU-intensive code paths as well as memory allocation hotspots, often indicating inefficient resource use or leaks.

To generate a CPU profile, the application can import net/http/pprof and expose profiling endpoints via HTTP. Example integrated usage is as follows:

```
import (
    _ "net/http/pprof"
    "log"
    "net/http"
)

func main() {
    go func() {
        log.Println(http.ListenAndServe("localhost:6060", nil))
    }()
    // Application logic here
}
```

Once running, profiles can be retrieved with:

```
go tool pprof http://localhost:6060/debug/pprof/profile?seconds=30
```

This command captures a 30-second CPU profile, which can then be analyzed interactively or converted to various formats for visual inspection. Heap profiles are similarly accessed at /debug/pprof/heap. Examining heap allocations reveals objects retaining memory, aiding detection of leaks or excessive allocation rates.

Detailed profiling reports allow navigation through calling stacks, enabling pinpointing of inefficient functions or patterns. Annotations expose inlining decisions, aiding developers to reduce call overhead or improve cache locality.

Beyond CPU and memory profiling, Go's runtime/trace package offers a mechanism for tracing program execution over time at the granularity of goroutine scheduling, syscall blocking, garbage collection, and network blocking. Tracing produces a timeline view of the application behavior, indispensable for diagnosing concurrency issues and latency bottlenecks.

To activate tracing, a program writes trace data to a destination, for example:

```
import (
    "os"
    "runtime/trace"
    "log"
)

func main() {
    f, err := os.Create("trace.out")
    if err != nil {
        log.Fatalf("failed to create trace output file: %v", err)
    }
    defer f.Close()

    if err := trace.Start(f); err != nil {
        log.Fatalf("failed to start trace: %v", err)
    }
    defer trace.Stop()

    // Application logic here
}
```

The resulting `trace.out` file can be examined with:

```
go tool trace trace.out
```

This opens a web-based UI allowing inspection of goroutine states, network delays, system events, and garbage collector pauses. Analyzing traces reveals synchronization delays, contention, and other anomalies affecting throughput or latency, which might be invisible from profiling alone.

For real-time monitoring, Go enables exposing internal metrics through HTTP in a structured manner compatible with monitoring systems like Prometheus. The expvar package can be used to publish key runtime statistics, counters, and custom metrics:

```
import (
    "expvar"
    "net/http"
)

var requests = expvar.NewInt("requests_total")

func handler(w http.ResponseWriter, r *http.Request) {
```

```
    requests.Add(1)
    w.Write([]byte("Hello, world!"))
}

func main() {
    http.HandleFunc("/", handler)
    http.ListenAndServe(":8080", nil)
}
```

This exposes a /debug/vars endpoint containing JSON-formatted statistics, which can be queried or scraped regularly. By enriching these metrics with application-specific counters, latencies, and gauges, operations teams gain continuous insight into runtime health and behavioral trends.

Interpreting profiling and tracing outputs focuses on identifying resource contention points and disproportional time or memory expenditure. Bottlenecks often stem from hot functions, excessive locking, unbalanced goroutine workload distribution, or blocking on I/O or synchronization primitives.

Key indicators include:

- High CPU percentage in a small subset of functions, signaling CPU-bound tasks that may benefit from algorithmic improvements or parallelization.

- Heap profiles indicating large or growing memory allocations, potential garbage collector pressure, or memory leaks.

- Trace views showing prolonged goroutine blocking or scheduling delays, suggesting synchronization inefficiencies or thread starvation.

- Elevated blocking profile counts that can highlight lock contention or long waiting times.

Addressing bottlenecks requires an iterative approach: profiling to detect, modifying code or architecture, then re-profiling to validate improvements. Performance tuning may involve changing data structures, adjusting concurrency patterns, reducing allocations, or fine-tuning runtime parameters such as garbage collector pacing and scheduler behavior.

The Go runtime exposes several environmental variables and configuration knobs that impact performance and reliability. Key parameters include:

- GOMAXPROCS: Controls the maximum number of CPUs that can execute simultaneously. Setting this to match available CPUs typically optimizes throughput, but performance may benefit from fine adjustments in specific workloads.

- Garbage collector tuning: The GODEBUG environment variable enables setting gcpercent to adjust aggressiveness of garbage collection relative to allocation rate, balancing latency and memory footprint.

- Scheduler tracing: Using GODEBUG=schedtrace= and schedtimetype= facilitates monitoring scheduler behavior and detecting excessive preemption or starvation.

Integrating profiling, tracing, and live diagnostics into routine development and operations cycles enables early detection of regressive behavior and promotes stable, performant releases. Continuous monitoring combined with thorough post-mortem analysis of anomalies enforces reliability while maintaining resource efficiency.

A pragmatic workflow involves:

1. Enabling pprof handlers in development and staging environments to periodically capture CPU and heap profiles.

2. Collecting runtime traces during performance tests or live diagnosis sessions to identify temporal issues and concurrency dynamics.

3. Publishing real-time metrics via `expvar` or Prometheus exporters for alerting and long-term trend analysis.

4. Examining collected data using `go tool pprof` and `go tool trace` along with graphical tools like `pprof` web interfaces or third-party profilers.

5. Applying targeted optimizations iteratively, guided by measurement rather than intuition.

Through mastery of these techniques, developers and operators can achieve deep visibility into Go application behavior, enabling informed decisions for tuning that elevate both performance and reliability.

9.7. Language Evolution and Compatibility

The Go programming language exemplifies a deliberate and disciplined approach to language evolution, emphasizing stability and compatibility to support long-lived software systems. This philosophy drives both the core language development and the growth of its extensive standard library, assuring developers that programs will remain reliable and maintainable over time.

At the heart of Go's evolution process lies a commitment to a strong compatibility guarantee: programs that compile and run successfully under one version of the language are expected to continue doing so on future releases. This promise profoundly influences the design and integration of new features, as any backward-incompatible change risks fracturing the extensive ecosystem of Go code.

To maintain this, Go employs a strict policy of never removing or changing the semantics of existing language constructs or standard library APIs in breaking ways. One consequence is that deprecated features remain available, allowing old codebases to function unchanged, while new code can adopt improved idioms. This approach contrasts with other modern languages that favor more rapid, sometimes disruptive, innovation at the expense of compatibility.

New language capabilities in Go are introduced through a rigorous proposal process, conducted via the Go language design discussions hosted openly on forums such as the golang-dev mailing list and the language's official issue tracker. Proposed changes undergo scrutiny for necessity, clarity, and impact on the overall ecosystem. Experimental or tentative features may first appear as opt-in or behind build flags, providing early access for feedback without affecting the default behavior.

A notable example is the gradual introduction of generics in Go 1.18. This language enhancement, years in design, was enabled by developing a type parameter system that integrates smoothly with existing interfaces and concrete types, enhancing expressivity while preserving the performance model and simplicity crucial to Go's appeal. The backward compatibility was ensured by maintaining the prior syntax and semantics for non-generic code, allowing existing programs to continue unaltered.

Feature previews and refinement continue beyond initial releases, often facilitated by Go's module system and versioning practices. The module proxy and version-awareness enable developers to specify precise library versions, making dependency management more predictable even as libraries evolve. This ecosystem-level version control complements language stability guarantees to offer a reliable development experience throughout complex dependency trees.

Library evolution is similarly conservative and incremental. The Go standard library grows by introducing new packages or extending existing ones with additional functionality only after demonstrated widespread need and careful API design. Interface changes within the standard library never break existing consumers. When

229

new methods or interfaces are added, they coexist alongside prior interfaces, preserving the behavioral contracts upon which programs rely.

An effective mechanism for enhancing the language without compromising compatibility is the use of `go:generate` directives and build constraints. These allow for optional tooling and code generation that can augment program capabilities dynamically and conditionally. Such techniques remain orthogonal to the core language and its runtime, enabling richer functionality while the language core and standard library remain stable.

The Go team also carefully manages language specification updates, which may clarify ambiguous wording or formally document behaviors exhibited by production implementations, but do not alter existing language dynamics. This meticulous documentation evolution prevents subtle regressions and ensures consistent compiler behavior across versions.

During the process of language evolution, stability commitments impact performance considerations as well. Any new feature or optimization introduced must maintain or improve efficiency without imposing burdensome runtime costs or bloating binaries. The Go compiler and runtime continue to benefit from rigorous benchmarking to validate that new additions do not erode the language's well-known speed and resource economy.

Go's language and standard library evolve through a combination of rigorous community collaboration, exacting design principles, and careful release management, all while upholding a steadfast guarantee of backward compatibility. This strategic progression ensures that Go remains a stable, reliable foundation for software development even as it embraces modern programming paradigms and capabilities, harmonizing innovation with production resilience.

www.ingramcontent.com/pod-product-compliance
Lightning Source LLC
Chambersburg PA
CBHW061246220326
41599CB00028B/5550